Mysterious Creatures

Mysterious Creatures

By the Editors of Time-Life Books

TIME-LIFE BOOKS, ALEXANDRIA, VIRGINIA

CONTENTS

A Gallery of Fabled Beasts

Real or imagined, strange creatures have walked the earth, swum in its seas, and winged through its skies from time immemorial; striking terror and awe in their beholders. And over many centuries, some of the most ferocious of these monsters have become firmly entrenched in legend, standing as vivid testimony to the human imagination.

Incredible as such creatures may seem, it is generally believed that they were based loosely on actual beasts—some of which were themselves known only through the reports of travelers and explorers returned from far-off lands. The griffin, a medieval invention that was said to live in some distant country, is a fanciful amalgam of the lion and the eagle. More than one fictitious monster was modeled after the snake, an animal long equated with evil in Western civilization. Almost certainly, the snake was the basis for the fire-breathing dragon, a creature onto which bat's wings and lizard's limbs appear to have been grafted. Scholars have further speculated that the remains of extinct animals, such as those of woolly mammoths and cave bears, might have inspired the creation of such monsters.

If the precise source of mythical monsters is a mystery, so is the motivation for conjuring up such creatures. Perhaps they were a convenient way to represent a civilization's innermost fears and fantasies or a means of explaining natural phenomena for which there were no obvious causes. Portraits of some of those extraordinary beings of myth and legend appear on the following pages.

The Fearsome and Fiery Dragon

Winged dragons made their first Western appearances in the works of ancient Greece and in the Bible, but it was medieval Europe whose imagination was most captured by the stubby-legged, fire-breathing monsters. As legend had it, any of those terrifying creatures, often having formidable horns, horrible fangs, and pestilential breath, might hold a town hostage and devour young virgins until it was killed by a virtuous knight, usually armed with a magical sword. The most famous hero to rescue a town and maiden was Saint George,

whose victory was seen as an allegory for Christianity's triumph over the powers of darkness. Dragons also loomed large in Chinese folklore, where they were relatively benign. But in the West they were evil; the real-life model for the fictional vampire Dracula, the prince Vlad Tepes, was nicknamed Dracula after the Romanian word for dragon and devil. Even in death, a dragon reportedly had extraordinary powers. A drop of its blood could kill instantly, and its teeth, planted in the earth, sprang up overnight as armed men.

The Man-Faced Manticore

Reputed to prowl the jungles of India, the fearsome manticore had the body of a lion, the face of a man, and the stinging tail of a scorpion. Its huge jaws, however, were unique: They held three rows of razor-sharp teeth, upper and lower, that interlocked like the teeth of a comb when the beast closed its mouth. The teeth could slash nearly anything to ribbons, and the manticore was said to relish feasting on humans. The monster was dangerous from afar as well. With its strangely segmented tail, it could fire lethal stingers that traveled as much as a hundred feet.

The Deceptive Kraken

The Kraken of Scandinavian lore was a horned sea monster so huge that it was sometimes mistaken for a group of islands by unsuspecting sailors who ventured far from shore. But when curious mariners drew near, the islands might erupt into a mass of multiple heads, horns, and waving tentacles that could grasp and sink even the largest of ships. The Kraken was also known to discharge an inky liquid that blackened and poisoned the waters—a characteristic that, like its tentacles, reveals the creature to be a monster-size version of the real-life giant squid.

The Baleful Basilisk

Of all the legendary monsters, none was deadlier than the basilisk, or cockatrice. Part
serpent, part rooster, it came from an egg laid by a seven-year-old cock during
the time that Sirius was high in the heavens. The egg was spherical and covered by
a thick membrane, and sometimes it was hatched by a toad, who sat on it
for nine years. This elaborate gestation produced a creature whose breath could
scorch the earth and whose glance was lethal—even to itself.
Accordingly, anyone who sought to slay the basilisk was wise to carry a mirror.

The Many-Headed Hydra

Said to lurk in swamps and other such watery realms, the hydra was a grotesque creature with at least seven independent heads—the center one of which was immortal—and an alarming ability to grow more. For every head that was lopped off by an adversary, the hydra grew two in its place. But this hideous beast was finally destroyed by Hercules, who buried the immortal head under a rock and burned off the others. The ancient Greeks probably got their inspiration for the mythical hydra from the octopus, which can regenerate lost tentacles.

The Gigantic Griffin

Half lion and half eagle, the griffin was far more formidable than either of those
beasts. It had the body and tail of a lion but was eight times as large; it had
an eagle's head and wings but was a hundred times stronger. This bizarre creature
was thought to dwell in the mountains, from which it swooped down on its
prey; with powerful talons the beast could carry back to its nest a horse and rider—it
was said to have a ravenous appetite for both—or even a pair of oxen
yoked together. Sometimes, griffins were themselves used for transport by the gods;

the chariot that bore Nemesis, the ancient Greeks' dreaded goddess of vengeance,
was frequently drawn by griffins. Naturally enough, humans were well
advised to avoid the beast at all costs. But it was so powerful that parts of its body
were greatly prized as talismans against evil and misfortune. Especially
sought after were its claws, the size of oxen horns, which were said to darken at the
merest touch of poison. During the Middle Ages, antelope horns or the
tusks of extinct mammoths were often sold to the gullible as griffins' claws.

CHAPTER 1

Creatures of the Sea

On the afternoon of October 31, 1983, a construction crew in Marin County, California, was hard at work on a coastal cliffside, repairing a stretch of Highway 1. Beneath them lay the sandy expanse of Stinson Beach and the vast waters of the Pacific. Shortly before two o'clock, a flagman on the crew turned away from his post and peered out to sea: He had spotted something very large and very strange speeding through the water toward the shore. The flagman quickly radioed a fellow worker, Matt Ratto, to grab his binoculars and take a closer look.

Up to then, the most interesting sight the binoculars had yielded was an occasional nude sunbather on the beach below. But now, through the field glasses, Ratto observed a gigantic, dark animal just a quarter of a mile away from his bird's-eye vantage point. It was like nothing he had ever seen before—a hundred feet long and quite thin, with three vertical humps or coils. On an otherwise ordinary autumn afternoon, Matt Ratto suddenly found himself staring at what looked, for all the world, to be a sea serpent.

As he watched, the creature picked its head up out of the water, appearing to look around. Then it reversed its direction, turning sharply and submerging its head, and swam back out to sea. Another witness, a truck driver named Steve Bjora, estimated its speed at forty-five to fifty miles an hour. To Bjora, who saw only two humps, the creature resembled a long eel.

A total of five workers viewed the spectacle that day, and their descriptions were in agreement concerning the beast's great length, slimness, and dark color. Another witness, transportation safety inspector Marlene Martin, possibly hoping to avoid ridicule, refused to discuss the sighting publicly. According to her daughter, however, Martin had indeed observed the creature and had described it to her family as a four-humped beast—the biggest thing that she had ever seen.

Yet another witness, nineteen-year-old Roland Curry, caught a glimpse of the serpent from the beach that afternoon. Later, he told reporters excitedly that it was the second time he had sighted the beast in less than a week. He had mentioned the first incident to his girlfriend but then let the matter drop after she told him that he was "nuts." Now, having seen the creature again with other witnesses present, he was convinced it was real.

Three days after the Stinson Beach sighting, a group of surfers spotted a similar monster more than 400 miles to the south, near Costa Mesa. Young Hutchinson, a twenty-nine-year-old surfer, said it emerged from the waters off the Santa Ana River jetty just ten feet from his board. At first Hutchinson was reluctant to speak of the incident, thinking that it was "too crazy." But after reading about the Marin County sightings, he came forward, confirming that the creature was just as the highway workers had described it—"a long black eel."

Throughout the century, there had been periodic sightings of mysterious creatures off the Pacific coast, but no one had ever been able to determine what they were. Scientists speculated that the 1983 apparitions may have been the distorted silhouettes of whales backlighted by the sun; others suggested that the beasts might have been lines of jumping porpoises. Ratto and Hutchinson scorned these logical explanations. Both of them knew what whales looked like, and they were positive that the thing they had seen was not a whale.

Of course, it is possible that Ratto, Hutchinson, and the others happened upon some sort of known phenomenon and simply failed to recognize it. Perhaps the October 31 sightings were Halloween hoaxes or mass hallucinations. Perhaps news coverage colored the vision of the later witnesses, causing them to see a phantom serpent in every swell or to indulge their fantasies of involvement in a big event. On the other hand, the Stinson Beach and Costa Mesa witnesses really may have seen an unknown marine monster—even an isolated species from the earth's far dis-

tant past. As one biologist reflected at the time, "there may be all sorts of prehistoric creatures swimming around out there that we know nothing about."

A monster is by definition anything that fails to conform to general views of what is normal—anything too strange, too large, too ugly, too evil, or too terrifying to be "real." Since the dawn of history, people have been beguiled and repelled by tales of legendary monsters—large, hidden animals, known to individuals or local populations but not to the world at large. Monsters have captured the imagination of poets, clerics, mariners, scientists, and ordinary citizens and fueled the ambitions of charlatans and attention seekers. Yet these creatures have persistently eluded their human hunters, seeming to secrete themselves in the earth's most remote and mysterious regions: oceans and seas, rivers and lakes, mountains and forests.

The vast, largely unexplored oceans have always been considered a breeding ground for strange creatures—identified and unidentified. Ancient mapmakers depicted seas teeming with beasts of every description—spiny, winged, horned, sharp-toothed, many-tentacled. Some of these, like the giant squid, have made the transition from mythical fancy to zoological fact. Others, generally called sea serpents—whether or not they are actually reptiles—still await scientific discovery.

Meanwhile, the deepest reaches of inland rivers and lakes are the reputed domain of great freshwater beasts such as the Loch Ness monster, or Nessie, and of Ogopogo, Champ, and Morag—many of them named for the bodies of water they haunt. And on land, remote mountains and forests around the world supposedly conceal huge, hairy, humanlike creatures with names like Yeti—the so-called

This sea devil was allegedly caught in the Adriatic in the 1400s.

English lore tells of a sea dragon.

Inspired by mariners' tales of encounters with exotic creatures, artists over the centuries have made images of the monsters—real or imaginary—that lurk in the sea. A sampling of their often fanciful drawings appears on these pages.

Abominable Snowman—Almas, Yowie, and Sasquatch, also known as Bigfoot.

While all of these reputed sea, lake, and land monsters have abundant natural hiding places, the oceans are certainly the widest, deepest, and most difficult to explore. These great bodies of water hold many mysteries and only grudgingly yield clues—many purely by chance. Even the most gigantic of beasts, after all, would be a microscopic drop in the vast bucket of the world's oceans, bays, and estuaries.

Most undersea exploration has been limited to the

This prickly creature was called a fish pig.

relatively narrow and shallow continental shelves that surround the major bodies of land. These shelves account for only seven percent of all underwater territory and do not even hint at the topographical variety of deeper regions: the precipitous continental slopes, the deep canyons and gullies, the gentle continental rises, and the flat, desertlike abyssal plain. This plain, 12,000 feet below sea level on average, covers nearly half the earth's surface. Relieving the monotony are occasional chasms, or trenches. The most spectacular, the Mindanao trench off the Philippines, plunges to depths of about 36,000 feet. And rising from the center of the two-mile-deep plain is the earth's largest mountain range—the 10,000-foot-high midocean ridge that winds some 35,000 miles underneath three major oceans.

Almost everything known about this underwater world is the result of recent technology. Using sophisticated sonar equipment, oceanic cartographers have produced detailed maps that show and even name most of the subaqueous regions and formations. But scientists have yet explored only minute fractions of all the oceans' depths firsthand and thus have little idea of what life-forms may be lurking in the watery plains, trenches, mountains, and valleys. Over the past few decades, sizable "new" aquatic creatures—having escaped human detection for thousands of years—have been steadily coming to light.

The study of previously unknown species—of the land and air as well as the sea—is known as cryptozoology, literally, the science of hidden animals *(page 20)*. Among the most spectacular modern finds was a creature that, though not a sea serpent, was indeed a prehistoric marine monster. The series of chance events leading to its discovery began in December of 1938, when fishermen aboard a South African trawler noticed a decidedly strange creature flopping amid the ordinary catch hauled from the waters of the Indian Ocean. Indeed, the large, dark blue fish with armorlike scales and huge blue eyes was so unusual that the trawler's owners presented it to Marjory Courtenay-Latimer, curator of the natural history museum in East London, South Africa. Unable to identify the fish, she wrote to Professor J. L. B. Smith at Rhodes University, enclosing a sketch. Unfortunately, the heavy volume of Christmas mail delayed the letter for several weeks, by which time the curator had had the fish mounted in order to preserve it; the internal organs had disappeared in the trash.

Nevertheless, the professor identified the creature as a coelacanth—a fish that had

The enormous squirting whale resembled an island.

lived 300 million years before and had been presumed extinct for nearly 70 million years. Smith named the discovery *Latimeria chalumnae* and published his findings, instantly creating a worldwide sensation. The scientific community hailed his single mutilated specimen as the find of the century. Professor Smith, however, could not be satisfied without a complete coelacanth. Printing leaflets in

This sinuous, bat-winged sea dragon resembles a flying eel.

Multiple eyes dot a piglike fish.

three languages, he offered a reward of 100 British pounds for each of the next two intact specimens.

One world war and fourteen years later, the professor found his second coelacanth. A fisherman named Ahmed Hussein had caught the fish in sixty-five feet of water near the shore of Anjuan, one of the Comores Islands located off the coast of Mozambique. All the islanders were familiar with the rare creature: They called it *kombessa* and considered it an edible but not particularly tasty meal. Hussein might well have eaten or sold his catch, but he chanced to meet a teacher who remembered the professor's leaflets, with their promise of a reward worth three years' income by the islanders' economic standards. So it was that the men got word to Professor Smith. Although this fish too was damaged, it did contain most of the internal organs. More important, it established the coelacanth's natural habitat and led to subsequent discoveries.

In the annals of cryptozoology, the history of the coelacanth is

A creature with a wild mane rears up and spews forth water from its dual spouts.

a classic success story: A hidden animal turns up by chance, falls into the right hands, and attracts instant scientific acclaim. And the fact that the coelacanth was presumed extinct was a special boon for sea-monster researchers—for if this prehistoric fish could survive undetected to modern times, might not any number of other ancient marine creatures do the same?

Another, more arduous, success story is that of the giant squid, which endured millennia of legend, centuries of ridicule, and decades of limbo before gaining identity as a scientific reality. The matter of the closely related giant octopus, on the other hand, has not yet reached its conclusion. At present the creature remains in the half-light of quasi recognition.

Although both of these cephalopods (from the ancient Greek for *head* and *foot*) are characterized by long, muscular arms lined with suckers and highly developed eyes, biol-

This whale was seen near Britain.

ogists see clear distinctions between the normal-size squid and octopus. Squid have ten arms, two of which are long, specialized tentacles, and they are active predators, with slender, streamlined bodies made for pursuing their victims. Octopuses are more bulbous shaped, have eight arms, and are more passive and reclusive, rarely leaving their ocean-floor lairs. However, in the legends passed on through the ages, the two giant versions of these cephalopods have been

A pig whale has walruslike tusks.

so inextricably intertwined and so frequently confused that it is sometimes hard to distinguish them. Often the creatures of ancient lore combine the characteristics of both—with a few whale traits thrown in for good measure.

The first known chronicler of the giant cephalopod

The Search for Unknown Beasts

Found off Hawaii in November 1976, this previously unknown shark was dubbed Mega-mouth. Another was netted off California in 1984.

A small band of biologists share a dream—to find species of sea or land animals hitherto completely unknown or to rediscover living examples of animals thought to have died out ages ago. Finds made in this century encourage these dreamers, whose field is aptly named cryptozoology—literally, the science of hidden animals.

Size and habitat are often responsible for an animal's having been overlooked. Not surprisingly, a bumblebee-size bat that lives in caves in Thailand eluded detection until 1973. But larger animals in less remote sites have also remained hidden. Herds of a species of peccary supposedly extinct since the last ice age, for instance, were found in Paraguay in 1975.

Native peoples sometimes offer scientists useful clues. An unusual feather in a local's hat sparked the discovery of a showy African peacock in 1936, and accounts of giant lizards on the Indonesian island of Komodo proved not to be mere myth when naturalist P. A. Ouwens identified four of the creatures captured in 1912. As cryptozoologists follow such leads into little-explored areas, they remain optimistic that it is not too late to uncover sensational surprises.

The 300-pound Komodo dragon has a 100-million-year history but has been known to science for less than a century.

The extremely rare giant panda is found only in China and Tibet. Westerners first saw a live one in the early 1900s.

Africa, a rich source of new species, yielded the giant forest hog of Kenya in 1904. No genus of large terrestrial mammal has been found since.

A member of the giraffe family, the shy okapi inhabits the rain forests of the Congo. It was unknown to science until around 1900.

Its remote habitat in the rain forest of central equatorial Africa's volcanic highlands protected the shy, shaggy-coated mountain gorilla from discovery until 1901.

was the poet Homer, who lived in the eighth or ninth century BC. In his *Odyssey,* he describes the horrific monster Scylla, who—despite her odd habit of yelping and her overabundance of feet, necks, and heads—appears to be a mythical embodiment of the giant octopus. Like the octopus, she awaits her prey "hid in the depth of the cavern." However, Scylla's "teeth in a threefold order" sound more like rows of a squid's serrated suckers than an octopus's smooth ones.

Medusa, another of Greek mythology's hideous monsters, may also be a giant cephalopod. Her hair of writhing snakes may well have represented arms, which in both octopus and squid appear to grow directly out of the head. Medusa's stare, which turned men to stone, calls to mind the huge, malevolent, almost-human eyes of the giant squid, possibly also of the giant octopus. In one dramatic twentieth-century encounter with a huge squid, a deep-sea salvage diver recounted how he was almost hypnotized, so enthralled was he by the creature's eyes—"eyes which seemed to concentrate in their gaze everything malignant and hateful." Only the squid's sudden movement brought the diver to his senses so that he could escape.

In the period preceding the Middle Ages, the giant cephalopod emerged, in combination with the whale, as the "island beast"—a monster so enormous that unwitting mariners would mistakenly land on it, only to discover, much to their dismay, that their island was moving. The Scandinavian counterpart, the Kraken, was first mentioned in a manuscript around AD 1000 and continued to figure in Norse legend for many centuries.

One particularly imaginative Norse tale was of a bishop who spotted an island he had never seen before and had his men row him there. He put ashore and celebrated an entire Mass to consecrate the new land. When he left, he was amazed to see the island vanish.

Centuries later, in 1752, another Scandinavian bishop published a major work on sea monsters. In his *Natural History of Norway,* Eric Ludvigsen Pontoppidan, bishop of Bergen, described the Kraken as "round, flat, and full of arms, or branches." The creature's flexible back reportedly measured a full English mile and a half in circumference, appearing at first to be a number of separate small islands, and its arms were sometimes as long as "masts of middle-sized vessels." Pontoppidan further described the monster as capable of sinking great ships—a deed long attributed to the giant squid.

At the beginning of the nineteenth century, giant cephalopods claimed one academic victim—at least figuratively. The French naturalist Pierre Denys de Montfort, fascinated by the rumored monsters, conducted extensive research on reported sightings and on remains found in the stomachs of sperm whales. In 1802 he published his *Histoire Naturelle des Mollusques,* but the work did more to set back the cause of serious research than to advance it. Denys de Montfort was undiscriminating in his choice of material, citing stories so sensationalistic and presenting illustrations so exaggerated that the scientific community ridiculed, denigrated, and ostracized him. He ended his days in poverty and literally died in the gutter, on a street in Paris.

Nevertheless, in the mid-nineteenth century, Danish zoologist Johan Japetus Steenstrup dared to readdress the Kraken-squid issue, collecting a great deal of information on recent sightings and beachings. In 1847 he delivered a paper on the subject to the Society of Scandinavian Naturalists. Steenstrup's reputation had already suffered greatly from an earlier error he had made, denying the coexistence of early humans and the woolly mammoth, and he might well have shared Denys de Montfort's ignominious end. But luck was with him. Scientifically acceptable evidence began to accumulate, and Steenstrup obtained the enormous pharynx and beak of a giant squid that had washed up on a Danish beach in 1853. At last, in 1857, he was able to publish a scientific description of *Architeuthis dux,* as the creature was named.

Although the giant squid had acquired an official title, some scientists continued to question its existence. Then came a sensational but reliable sighting. On November 30, 1861, the French gunboat *Alecton* spotted a giant squid near

A villager from Comoro Island, off the coast of Mozambique, displays a coelacanth. Until one was caught in 1938, the ancient fish had been presumed extinct for 70 million years. The find prompted scientists to wonder what other living relics might be swimming in the oceans.

Teneriffe, in the Canary Islands. The commander, Lieutenant Frédéric Marie Bouyer, decided to capture it. His men shot at the beast, but to no avail. After a long struggle, they managed to harpoon it and slip a rope around it. However, as they tried to haul the body aboard, it broke apart; all but the end of the tail fell back into the water. When the *Alecton* reached Teneriffe, Bouyer showed the tail to the French consul and made an official report to the navy. A month later a paper on the incident was presented to the French Academy of Sciences. Some hard-core skeptics remained unconvinced, but in the 1870s so much evidence turned up on the beaches of Newfoundland and Labrador that there ~~could~~ no longer be any doubt of the giant squid's existence. ~~For un~~known reasons, a large number of the creatures be~~came stranded a~~nd wash ashore. Some wound up as dog food or ~~sc~~ience got its share.

~~One of~~ these squid ever recognized by science ~~was one~~ that appeared near the beach of Thimble

Tickle, Newfoundland, in 1878. On November 2, Stephen Sperring and two companions were out fishing when they saw a massive object close to the shore. Assuming that it was part of a shipwreck, they approached—only to discover a thrashing, glassy-eyed squid, aground in the shallow waters of an ebb tide. The three men hooked the disabled beast with a grapnel and towed it to shore, where they tied it to a tree to keep it from washing back out to sea. The magnificent specimen had a twenty-foot body and a thirty-five-foot tentacle, giving it an overall length of fifty-five feet. Its eyes are thought to have measured eighteen inches across, its suckers four inches. The men hacked it up for dog food, but not before it was examined by a local clergyman, Moses Harvey, who attested to the discovery in a letter to a Boston newspaper.

The oceans may conceal squid several times the size of the Thimble Tickle monster. Eighteen-inch sucker scars on whale carcasses seem to indicate the existence of squid more than 120 feet in length. But the evidence is unclear, since scars grow at the same time a whale grows.

If acceptance of the giant squid was a long time in coming, progress has been far slower and more stubborn in the case of its cousin, the elusive giant octopus. Indeed, we may never be able to determine which—if any—of the Kraken-squid tales and sightings actually involved octo-puses. The fact remains that, to date, the entire body of physical evidence consists of a single find— rejected in its day, forgotten for about half a century, finally identified in the 1950s, and yet to receive universal recognition.

The chance discovery took place on November 30, 1896, when two boys cycling on Anastasia Beach, near St. Augustine, Flori-da, came upon a partially bur-ied, gargantuan carcass. Dr. De-Witt Webb, a physician with an avid interest in natural history, examined the badly decom-posed body and concluded that it was a giant octopus. The ex-posed part alone was twenty-three feet long and eighteen feet wide; fragments of the arms, which were discovered a few days later, measured up to thirty-two feet in length.

Webb wrote to several sci-entists about the find, and one of his letters reached a noted cephalopod expert, Yale profes-sor A. E. Verrill. Without actually seeing the remains, Verrill im-mediately identified the creature as a squid. However, on the ba-

French naturalist-artist Pierre Denys de Montfort's pench[...]lt fo[...] sationalism magnifies a[...]n octop[...] unbelievably colossa[...] size as i[...] a hapless ship. He[...] apparentl[...] his illustration o[...]n a story e[...] told of an encou[...]ter with[...] sea creature off t[...]he coas[...]

Amateur naturalist DeWitt Webb poses in 1896 with what he concluded was the remains of a giant octopus. Webb had used ropes to haul the carcass onto the beach again after it had washed out to sea.

sis of further information and photographs, he changed his mind, publishing articles that described and officially named *Octopus giganteus*. By his calculations, the creature had tentacles between seventy-five and 100 feet long. But then, after examining tissue samples Webb had cut from the mantle and body, Verrill changed his mind yet again, retracting his identification and declaring the tissue to be from the head and nose of a whale.

The matter was laid to rest until one day in 1957, when Forrest Glen Wood, a marine biologist at Marineland of Florida, came across an old clipping that told of the St. Augustine monster. Intrigued, he began to research the subject, digging up old photos, drawings, articles, and let-

discovered that the Smithsonian Institution in

sonian tissues, which he examined along with cuttings from known octopuses and squid. At first, he could not discern any cellular structure at all. However, when examined under polarized light, the connective tissues revealed distinct structural differences. Gennaro found that the pattern of the St. Augustine sample was unlike that of any known whale or squid but was quite similar, though not identical, to that of known octopuses. More recently, Roy P. Mackal, a biochemist with a wide-ranging interest in cryptozoology, has performed amino-acid analyses reinforcing the theory that the St. Augustine monster was an octopus.

Although these findings have been questioned or ignored by many authorities, Wood and a few other experts continue to believe that the giant octopus lives somewhere in the deep Bahamian waters, perhaps near Andros Island, such a creature abound. Diving expedi- up any evi- but searchers believe that they may still be lurking in the deeper waters of the nearby trench known as the Tongue of the Ocean—or perhaps off the west coast of Bermuda.

To some cryptozoologists, the scattered evidence of the giant octopus and the firm reality of the giant squid have opened up endless new prospects. If these once-mythical monsters really exist, they ask, then is the legendary sea serpent really so far beyond the realm of possibility?

Sea serpents have long inspired fascination, terror—and snorts of derision. Their association with myth, religious symbolism, sensationalism, and naive credulity has largely consigned these creatures to scientific exile. However, during the eighteenth century—the Age of Enlightenment—a great increase in travel, trade, and intellectual inquiry produced a significant change in the quality of testimony.

Probably the first of the modern eyewitnesses was the Scandinavian missionary Hans Egede, known as the Apostle of Greenland. A reputable, respected minister, he had a sharp eye for detail, an intense interest in natural history, and a no-nonsense attitude—in short, the qualities of an excellent witness. Egede reported that he sighted a sea monster on a 1734 voyage to Greenland, and his subsequent description of the creature was remarkable for its sober, matter-of-fact tone.

As portrayed in Egede's *Description of Greenland*, the sea serpent was certainly very large and unusual, but it was no archetypal, fire-breathing, mariner-eating monster. The animal's head reached the top of the mast, but did not tower above or devour it. The body was as broad as the ship and three or four times as long. The minister described the creature as having paddlelike paws and a long, pointed snout and wrote that it spouted "like a whale-fish." The body was said to be covered with a carapace of shellwork, not scales; the lower portion was serpentine in shape, with the tail a "ship's length distant from the bulkiest part of the body." All in all, it seemed to be a description meant to inform and not to thrill. Yet even so, the skeptics could not accept it at face value.

In the early nineteenth century, the sea serpent did have a brief but glorious moment of respectability. Between August 6 and 23 of 1817, as many as a hundred reputable witnesses sighted an enormous marine monster frolicking in or near the harbor in Gloucester, Massachusetts. For a

Shown in a nineteenth-century engraving, the first sea serpent reported in the New World glides through the waters off Cape Ann, Massachusetts, in 1639. The monster supposedly slithered ashore and coiled itself.

In August 1817, a broadside published in Boston carried an electrifying story—a sea serpent had been seen repeatedly in Gloucester Harbor on Cape Ann, not far from the site where a similar creature had appeared some 180 years before. The alarm was first raised by two women who reportedly saw the monster enter the harbor on August 6. Some people believed the women had mistaken a line of sharks or porpoises for a sea serpent, but several fishermen soon corroborated their story. Over the course of three weeks, dozens of witnesses saw a round, multihumped serpent 50 to 100 feet long moving rapidly through the water. At month's end it vanished, although scattered sightings occurred over the next three years.

A Monstrous Sea Serpent,

The largest ever seen in America,

Has just made its appearance in Gloucester Harbour, Cape Ann, and has been seen by hundreds of Respectable Citizens.

The Editor of the Salem Gazette, says:—We have in our possession an extract of a letter from John Low, Esq. to his son in this town, dated Gloucester, Thursday afternoon, August 14, 1817.

"There was seen on Monday and on Tuesday morning playing about our harbor, between Eastern Point and Ten pound Island, a SNAKE with his head and body about eight feet out of water, his head is in perfect shape as large as the head of a horse, his body is judged to be about FORTY-FIVE OR FIFTY FEET IN LENGTH, it is thought he will girt about 3 feet round the body, and his sting is about 4 feet in length.

While writing the above a person has called in, who says that there are two to be seen, playing from the Stage-head into the harbor inside of Ten pound Island. The spectators are Mr. Charles Smith, Mr. John Proctor and several others. A number of our sharp shooters are in pursuit of him but cannot make a ball penetrate his head. Another party is just going in pursuit with guns, harpoons &c. Our small craft is fearful of venturing out a fishing.

The above can be attested to by twenty different people of undoubted veracity."

In addition to this account the Salem Register states, that the Serpent is extremely rapid in its motions which are in all directions, that it shews a length of 50 feet; that a man who discharged his musket within 30 feet of the Serpent, says its head was partly white and that he hit it, that a large sum had been offered for it; that "it appears in joints like wooden buoys on a net rope almost as large as a barrel, that musket balls appear to have no effect on it, that it appears like a string of gallon kegs 100 feet long."

The editor of the Register quotes an account of a Sea Serpent seen on the coast in 1746, something like it. It had a head like that of a horse, and as he moved he looked like a row of large casks following in a right line.

The Boston Daily Advertiser in speaking of this Monstrous Serpent, says—We have seen several letters from Gloucester, which describe a prodigious Snake that has made its appearance in Cape-Ann Harbour. It was first seen by some fishermen, 10 or 12 days ago, but it was then generally believed to be the creature of the imagination. But he has since come within the harbor of Gloucester, and has been seen by hundreds of people. He is declared by some persons who approached within 10 or 15 yards of him, to be 60 or 70 feet in length, round, and of the diameter of a barrel. Others state his length variously, from 50 to 100 feet. His motions are serpentine, extremely varied, and exceedingly rapid. He turns himself completely round almost instantaneously. He sometimes darts forward, with his head out of water, at the rate of a mile in 3 minutes, leaving a wake behind, of half a mile in length. His head, as large as the head of a horse, is shaped somewhat like that of a large dog, is raised about 8 feet out of water and is partly white, the other part black. He appears to be full of joints and resembles a string of buoys on a net rope, as is set in the water to catch herring. Others describe him as like a string of water casks. His back is black. Various attempts have been made, without success, to take him. Four boats went out on Thursday, filled with adventurous sailors and experienced gunners, armed with muskets, harpoons, &c. Three muskets were discharged at him from a distance of 30 feet, two balls were thought to hit his head, but without effect. He immediately after plunged into the water, and disappeared for a short time, after which he moved off to the outer harbor, and was seen no more that night. A number of persons are employed in making a net of cod-line, of sufficient size to take him. It is conjectured that he has resorted to this harbor for the purpose of preying upon a very numerous shoal of herrings, which have lately appeared there. If he has been instrumental, as is supposed, in driving these herring into the harbor, he has rendered an essential service to the town.

The Salem Gazette of the 19th inst. says, "We are informed, that on Sunday this creature was seen playing sometimes within 15 or 20 feet of the shore, affording a better opportunity to observe him than had before occured. Gentlemen from Gloucester state, that he appeared to them even of greater magnitude than had before been represented, and should judge from their own observation, that he was as much as 150 feet in length, and as big round as a barrel. They saw him open an enormous mouth, and are of opinion that he is cased in shell.

Aug. 22, 1817.

Printed and Sold by Henry Bowen, Devonshire-Street, Boston.

time skepticism all but disappeared; scientists throughout the world followed the story with avid interest.

On August 14 alone, the monster appeared to a group of twenty to thirty people, among them the Gloucester justice of the peace, Lonson Nash. That same day several boats went out in active pursuit, and late in the afternoon, a ship's carpenter, Matthew Gaffney, spotted "the strange marine animal, resembling a serpent." He got to within thirty feet of it, took careful aim with a rifle, and fired directly at the head. An experienced marksman, Gaffney thought he must have hit it, but the serpent appeared to be unharmed. It veered sharply toward the boat, and for a minute the men feared that the creature would attack. Instead, it simply sank like a stone, passed under the craft, and surfaced on the other side, almost a hundred yards away. There it continued to play, apparently heedless of the hunters.

Gaffney later described the monster as probably smooth skinned and certainly dark in color, with a white throat and belly. It was huge—at least forty feet long—and its head was the size of "a four-gallon keg." Moving vertically, "like a caterpillar," it was speeding along at between twenty and thirty miles per hour.

This and other eyewitness accounts were the result of an intensive investigation by a committee of the Linnaean Society of New England. Under the committee's direction, Justice of the Peace Nash issued a twenty-five-item questionnaire and took a number of depositions from firsthand witnesses only. The majority of the reports agreed in essence with Gaffney's description, and they provided additional information. Some of the other witnesses noted that the creature had a many-humped back (with as many as ten humps) and that it moved by undulating vertically. The head, held six to twelve inches above the water, resembled that of a snake or turtle.

Modern authorities agree that the Gloucester monster could not have been a snake; reptiles cannot undulate vertically or sink straight down. However, the Linnaean Society was apparently unaware of these facts. Believing that the sea serpent was indeed a snake, the society theorized that it

had come to lay eggs on shore. At one point, independent witnesses reported seeing it half on and half off the sandy beach of the harbor, which lent credence to the theory. No eggs ever turned up, but two boys found a three-foot creature that looked like a black snake with humps on its back. The society, sure of its egg-laying theory, was delighted with this apparent proof—the "baby sea serpent." The members examined and dissected it, then christened it *Scoliophis atlanticus*, or Atlantic Humped Snake, publishing a long report on the subject.

Europe greeted the find with extreme skepticism, and in little time a French zoologist, Charles-Alexandre Lesueur, had determined that the *Scoliophis* was just what it appeared to be: a black snake with a spine deformed by disease or injury. The international scientific community had a great laugh at the Linnaean Society's expense, and the whole Gloucester Harbor episode was discredited—damaging the case for other alleged sea serpents. Similar unidentified marine creatures continued to appear off the coasts of New England and Canada, but it would be many years before people would again take them seriously.

The Linnaean Society's blunder was a serious but honest error. However, other "errors" regarding sea serpents have been far less honest. Over the years, a number of deliberate sea-serpent hoaxes have been foisted upon a credulous public. Whether their perpetrators were indulging in personal fantasies, seeking attention, playing practical jokes, or attempting to cash in on serious scientific endeavor, most of the hoaxes were too farfetched or contradictory to hold up under scrutiny. The most spectacular and successful of the schemes was engineered by a German collector named Albert Koch, who opened an exhibit of a supposed sea-serpent skeleton in 1845 and fleeced gullible spectators on two continents before his exposure as a fraud *(page 30)*.

Such hoaxes soured serious-minded people on the subject of sea serpents. But in 1848, a sighting by several officers in the British navy shook the foundations of British

An Artful Patchwork Serpent

In 1845, New Yorkers drawn by news of a scientific sensation flocked to Broadway's Apollo Saloon. There, for the admission price of twenty-five cents, they could examine a 114-foot-long skeleton that was, according to sometime archaeologist and show organizer Albert Koch, the remains of an extinct marine reptile he had dug up on expedition to Alabama. With its slender form, undulating backbone, and threateningly reared head, Koch's creature bore a remarkable resemblance to the sea serpents that had been reported for two centuries in American waters. Many viewers went away satisfied that they had seen scientific proof of marine monsters.

Unfortunately for Koch, the Harvard-educated anatomist Jeffries Wyman visited the exhibit. After carefully inspecting the skeleton, he announced that it was a fraud. He noted that its teeth had the double roots characteristic of mammals but not of reptiles and went on to demonstrate that Koch's wonder was actually a composite of several specimens of an extinct whale, the zeuglodon. Koch had combined a jumble of bones cleverly, but not cleverly enough to fool an expert eye.

Angrily denying Wyman's conclusion, Koch packed up his serpent and took it to his native Europe, where he mounted his exhibit in city after city. His reputation had preceded him, however, and he was a laughingstock among European scientists. In the end, though, his brazen hoax turned out to be of some scholarly interest after all. In 1847, the king of Prussia bought Koch's fraudulent skeleton and added it to the collection of Berlin's Royal Anatomical Museum.

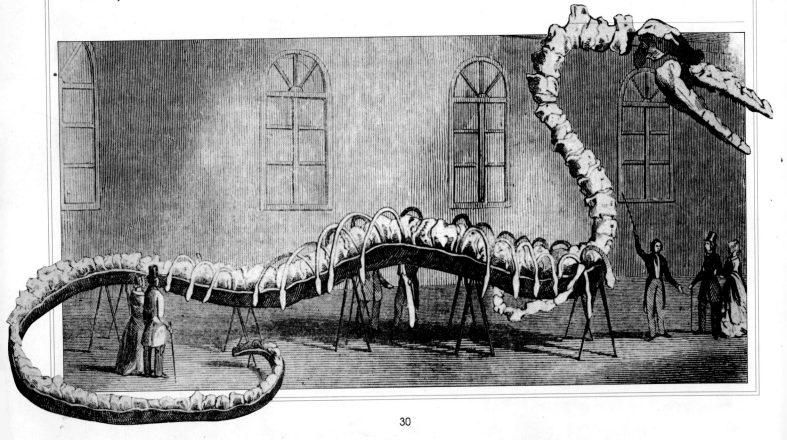

Apparently oblivious to the frigate Daedalus, a sea serpent passes under the ship's stern on a cloudy south Atlantic afternoon in August 1848. This engraving is based on a drawing commissioned by Captain Peter M'Quhae, one of seven eyewitnesses.

and European skepticism. On August 6, HMS *Daedalus* was cutting through the South Atlantic waters near the Cape of Good Hope, at the southern tip of Africa, when a midshipman spotted something advancing rapidly toward the vessel. He immediately informed the ship's officers, and a total of seven men, including Captain Peter M'Quhae, got a good view of what they all described as a gigantic sea serpent. The visible portion of the creature alone measured more than sixty feet in length, they reported, but it appeared to be only about fifteen inches in diameter. Its color was dark brown, with yellowish white at the throat, and it had some sort of mane, like a bunch of seaweed, on its back. Oddly enough, though moving at twelve to fifteen miles per hour, it exhibited neither vertical nor horizontal undulation—nor any other visible means of propulsion. "Apparently on some determined purpose," it held its serpentlike head a constant four feet above the surface and never deviated from its course.

When the *Daedalus* returned home to Plymouth and reports of the sighting appeared in the London *Times*, the lords of the Admiralty demanded a full account. M'Quhae wrote a detailed official report, which also appeared in the newspapers. Uproar ensued. While the sighting had been fairly typical, as sightings go, the credibility of the witnesses was unique. M'Quhae and his fellow officers commanded respect; the British, long used to thinking of the sea serpent as a figment of gullible imaginations, could not so easily dismiss the *Daedalus* monster. Having little choice but to accept the sincerity of the report, the doubters fell back on their mistaken-identity arguments, and the controversy raged in the press for some time.

Implicit in every such debate of that era was a basic indictment of the witnesses themselves. Even if their reputations were above reproach, their scientific capabilities were not. Mariners, priests, and ordinary travelers were deemed too unschooled in the principles of scientific observation to be able to judge the validity of what they were seeing. And despite centuries of reported sightings around

*On June 2, 1877, the officers and crew of H. M. S. Osborne saw
what they described as a monster in calm waters off northern Sicily. One witness
sketched the row of fins that first caught his eye (left) and a rear
view of the creature's head, shoulders, and flippers.*

the world, no trained scientist had ever caught so much as a glimpse of a sea monster. But this line of argument crumbled in 1905, when two respected naturalists, fellows of the London Zoological Society, sighted a huge, unidentified marine creature.

On December 7 of that year, naturalists E. G. B. Meade-Waldo and Michael J. Nicoll were cruising off Parahiba, Brazil, aboard the Earl of Crawford's yacht *Valhalla* when Meade-Waldo noticed a large, six-foot-long "fin or frill" in the water about a hundred yards from the boat. Looking more closely, he could see a large body beneath the surface. Just as he got out his binoculars, the scientist reported, a huge head and neck rose up out of the water. The visible portion of the neck alone was seven to eight feet long and as thick as "a slight man's body"; the head was about the same thickness and resembled a turtle's, as did the eye. Both head and neck were dark brown on top, whitish underneath.

Nicoll's account of the beast was similar to Meade-Waldo's, with one important addition: His general impression was of a mammal, not a reptile, although he admitted that he could not be absolutely certain.

Although these reports do not differ markedly from many other sea-monster sightings, they were less readily dismissed by scientists—although they certainly did not turn the tide of skepticism. Meade-Waldo and Nicoll were rare

exceptions. The myth-enshrouded monster has almost always brought ridicule upon its chroniclers and witnesses, many of whom have forever after rued the day they reported a sighting. It is impossible to estimate how many accounts have been lost when observers convinced themselves that they had had too much sun or one drink too many—or simply did not want to be ridiculed. The story is told of one sea captain who actually refused even to look at a sea serpent. He was having lunch in his cabin when the officer of the watch summoned him to the bridge to view a strange beast. The captain refused to go, refused even to peek out a porthole. "Had I said that I had seen the sea serpent," he explained, "I would have been considered a warranted liar all my life."

With the advent of powered vessels to take the place of sailing ships, reports of unknown or unidentified animals spotted on the high seas began to taper off. No longer at the mercy of whimsical winds and ocean currents, captains could steer their courses along established shipping lanes— and it is likely, say some cryptozoologists, that sea serpents and the like may stay away from these heavily traveled areas and thus avoid detection. Surely the clatter of engines would provide such creatures—if they exist—with ample warning of the presence of possible danger. In the words of the renowned Norwegian explorer Thor Heyerdahl: "We usually plow across [the sea] with roaring engines and piston strokes, with the water foaming round our bow. Then we come back and say that there is nothing to see far out on the ocean." Thus, it is not so surprising that most modern sightings appear to take place from the shore or from small boats near the shoreline.

For some reason, the California coast seems to be especially hospitable to modern monsters. In addition to the unidentified creatures spotted in 1983 at Stinson Beach and Costa Mesa, Cape San Martin has had a mystery visitor named Bobo, Monterey has had one dubbed the Old Man, and San Clemente has had its San Clemente monster—the most famous of them all.

First appearing between 1914 and 1919, this creature was sighted many times in the warm waters of the Outer Santa Barbara Channel, between San Clemente and Santa Catalina islands. Over the years members of the Tuna Club, the first American big-game fishing club, often observed

and reported the monster, enhancing its fame. Their descriptions were so consistent that one interviewer commented, "It was almost as though a recording had been made and each man played the same record." However, the writer added, "these men were all interviewed separately and none of them knew that I had talked to anyone else about the San Clemente monster." A skeptic might well wonder whether the club members had spent hour upon hour discussing the biggest fish story of them all, until their descriptions melded into a single composite version—but this question remains unanswered.

At some time between 1914 and 1919, Ralph Bandini, secretary of the club, saw the monster once, briefly and from a great distance. But in 1920 he got a relatively close look at it. As described in Bandini's 1932 book, *Tight Lines*, the creature had several remarkable features: a dark color; a long, thick, columnar neck; a mane that looked like fine seaweed or coarse hair; and enormous, protuberant eyes. The neck and head stood ten feet out of the water and were five or six feet in diameter. The round, bulging eyes were a good twelve inches in diameter—and horrifyingly dull and lifeless. Like so many other supposed sea serpents, this one submerged by sinking straight down. Having viewed only its head and neck, Bandini had to guess at its total size; he judged the creature to be larger than the

Naturalist Michael J. Nicoll and some colleagues glimpsed this long-necked, large-finned animal from a ship off Brazil one morning in 1905. Spotted again the following moonlit night by three crew members, the creature was, Nicoll asserted, an example of the "great sea-serpent" that had been reported so frequently.

largest whale, for the waves did not cause it to move, as they would a whale.

During World War II, most mariners were more concerned with enemy vessels than with sea serpents, and the creatures seem to have dropped out of sight for the duration of hostilities. The early postwar years were also relatively quiet ones for sea serpents, which had all but disappeared from the news except as occasional, lighthearted space fillers. Most people, if they thought about the creatures at all, thought of them as quaint mariners' folklore or crackpots' hallucinations. But then, at the end of 1947, came a report that a Grace Lines steamer, the *Santa Clara,* had run over a sea serpent, apparently injuring it severely.

A little before noon on December 30, the ship was moving uneventfully through calm waters 118 miles off Cape Lookout, North Carolina, when suddenly a huge serpent's head seemed to rear up just thirty feet from the bow. Three of the ship's officers were on the bridge at the time, and all three men had a close look at the creature as they passed over it. In an instant they had left it behind, thrashing wildly in the vessel's churning wake. They described an enormous beast with a head two feet across and five feet in length and a cylindrical body about three feet wide. The creature appeared to be smooth skinned and was dark brown.

Once more, reputable eyewitnesses had given a detailed description that seemed consistent with previous, similar testimony. But until the 1960s, the only evidence for sea-monster sightings remained just that: the subjective verbal accounts of those who said they had seen the creatures. Then, in early 1965, proof seemed to be at hand. A French photographer named Robert Le Serrec reported that he had taken the first real photographs of a sea serpent.

According to Le Serrec's story, his encounter occurred just off the coast of Queensland, Australia, on December 12, 1964. He was, he said, crossing the shallow waters of Stonehaven Bay in a small boat with his family and a friend, Henk de Jong, when his wife caught sight of a huge, peculiar object on the sandy bottom, less than six feet from the surface. De Jong at first thought it was a large, twisted tree trunk, but it soon became evident that this was some sort of monstrous creature—a creature shaped like a giant tadpole with an enormous head and tapering, serpentine body. Le Serrec took some still photos and then, circling his motorboat gradually closer, began to film it with a movie camera. As the boat drew near, the witnesses could make out a five-foot-long wound gouged open on the motionless animal's back and could more clearly see the broad head, which greatly resembled a snake's.

At this point the Le Serrec children became extremely frightened. The adults took the youngsters back to shore in the dinghy, then continued their observation of the beast. Since it remained inert, apparently seriously injured or perhaps even dead, they ventured still closer, noting two whitish eyes—located strangely on the top of the head—and regularly spaced bands of brown along the amazing length of the black body. The Le Serrecs and de Jong thought of trying to provoke the creature into moving but reconsidered, fearing that if it did move, it might smash the boat. Nevertheless, the men decided to dive for a better look, the photographer armed with an underwater camera and his companion with an underwater rifle.

Beneath the surface the water was murkier than it had appeared, and the divers could not get a clear view until they were within twenty feet of the monster. It was truly gigantic—seventy-five to eighty feet long, with four-foot-wide jaws and two-inch eyes that at close range turned out to be pale green. Suddenly, as Le Serrec began filming, the beast began to open and half-close its cavernous jaws "in a menacing manner" and to turn slowly toward the men. Because it was clearly incapacitated, the photographer kept on filming for a short time before he and his friend made their escape. Back aboard the boat, they discovered that the creature had disappeared. Le Serrec's wife had seen it swim out to sea, undulating horizontally—a motion typical of an eel or a reptile, not a mammal.

On February 4, 1965, Le Serrec released his story, instantly stirring up worldwide interest—and, of course, skep-

From Parson's Beach in Cornwall, England, Anthony "Doc" Shiels (left) points toward a spot in Falmouth Bay where he says he saw the sea serpent Morgawr in 1976. The same year, a woman known only as Mary F. allegedly took a photograph of this famous monster (below). Some investigators thought her picture genuine, but she aroused suspicion by refusing to give her full name or address and failing to submit the negative for examination.

ticism. This time, even such an adventurous cryptozoologist as the Scottish-born Ivan T. Sanderson, an author and naturalist with a wide-ranging interest in unusual wildlife, had grave doubts. Although Le Serrec's color photographs seemed genuine enough, his much-touted movies did not turn up for viewing by independent investigators, and rumor had it that they were hopelessly blurred and virtually useless. The sighting could not be explained on the basis of any known phenomenon, and investigators had to consider the definite possibility of an intentional hoax. Especially suspect, in the opinion of French-born cryptozoologist Bernard Heuvelmans, were the unique positioning of the animal's eyes, the handy removal of the children, who might have revealed the ruse, and the contradictory fact that the men were afraid to provoke the creature from the boat but not to approach it underwater.

Further disturbing facts emerged concerning Le Serrec himself. He was wanted by Interpol for leaving France, in 1960, with a lien on his yacht and for absconding with funds put up by would-be sailing companions, whom he left behind. Le Serrec had reportedly told them that he had an idea for bringing in a great deal of money—something "to do with the sea serpent."

When he finally returned to France in 1966, Le Serrec received a six-month jail sentence. Yet several months after his conviction, the magazine *Paris Match* printed his color photograph of the supposed sea serpent, attesting to the photographer's reliability and misquoting two experts—Sanderson and a professor named Paul Budker—in support of the Le Serrec claim. Although *Paris Match* did not print a retraction, a rival publication subsequently exposed the sighting as a hoax.

Not long afterward, photography once again figured in the case for a sea serpent in Britain's Falmouth Bay—a legendary Cornish beast that seems to have bridged the ages to become one of the most famous of modern monsters. *Morgawr*—the old Cornish word for "sea giant"—allegedly appeared once in 1876 and at least twice early in this century, but the witnesses' subjective verbal descriptions were considered vague, inconsistent, and generally far-fetched.

In 1975, a new flurry of sightings began, and in February of the following year, a woman publicly identified only as Mary F. produced a photograph. Accompanying the picture was a description of a fifteen- to eighteen-foot creature that looked to the photographer "like an elephant waving its trunk, but the trunk was a long neck with a small head on the end, like a snake's head." It was humpbacked, with multiple humps that moved "in a funny way," and had dark brown or black skin, "like a sea-lion's." The photograph showed no obvious signs of falsification, but the negative was never submitted for examination.

A professional magician and carnival entertainer named Anthony "Doc" Shiels was impressed by the Morgawr story and began to investigate the sightings. Because of his background as a showman, however, Shiels's findings have been regarded as highly questionable. Shiels believes that sea monsters are not merely unknown animals but beings that can be summoned through such means as witches' incantations and telepathy. In fact, on Easter of 1976 three self-proclaimed witches named Psyche, Vivienne, and Amanda attempted unsuccessfully to call up Morgawr by swimming naked in Falmouth Bay. But in November of 1980, Shiels's daughter Kate claimed to have succeeded by using the same technique.

Shiels says he has seen the creature himself on several occasions—once, in 1976, when he reportedly conjured it up in the company of David Clark, editor of *Cornish Life* magazine and a skeptic before the sighting. Since 1976, many people—including bankers, an art historian, fishermen, and members of a British Broadcasting Corporation film crew—have testified to seeing Morgawr.

Among the eyewitnesses were Sheila Bird, author of *Bygone Falmouth,* and her brother, Australian scientist Eric Bird, who was visiting her at the time. On the evening of July 10, 1985, the two were relaxing atop a cliff west of Portscatho, when Eric jumped up, startled. In the water below was a large, mottled gray creature with a long neck, small

World-renowned cryptozoologist Bernard Heuvelmans has written widely in the field. Among his books is In the Wake of the Sea-Serpents, *a definitive study of reported sightings of sea creatures from ancient times to the present.*

single or perhaps multiple humps. Morgawr is small for a sea serpent; like Bird, most witnesses have judged it to be between twelve and twenty feet long, although one report indicates a monster more than twice that length.

North America has also had its share of recent sightings, and not just on the California coast. For example, tourists and natives have repeatedly reported seeing Caddy, the so-called Vancouver Island monster—probably the northern counterpart of the maned San Clemente sea serpent. In 1969, a pair of marine scientists at the University of British Columbia—oceanographer Paul H. LeBlond and biologist John Sibert—launched a research project to ferret out unreported sightings of sea monsters in the area. The scientists prepared a questionnaire and sent it to all the newspapers on the British Columbia coast, as well as to marinas, fishing clubs, and lighthouse keepers. Responses quickly began arriving.

head, and huge hump. From their elevated vantage point, the brother and sister could also see a long, muscular tail beneath the surface of the water. The tail was about the same length as the body, and the creature appeared to be seventeen to twenty feet long in all. As the witnesses looked on in awe, Morgawr moved rapidly but regally through the water, its head held high, then suddenly submerged, dropping like a stone. Sheila Bird waited a month and a half to report the sighting, for it had taken place just as she was launching her book, and she feared that her account would be construed as a publicity gimmick.

Although the numerous Falmouth testimonies are not perfectly complete or consistent, together they provide a picture of a long-necked creature with a small head and

Typical of the matter-of-fact eyewitness stories LeBlond and Sibert received was one sent by a woman identified as Mrs. E. Stout, of Klamath Falls, Oregon. In March of 1961, Mrs. Stout testified, she was walking with her sister-in-law and their two preschool-age sons along the shore of the Strait of Juan de Fuca, which divides Washington State and British Columbia. The strollers were watching a freighter in the channel, and as the ship moved away, they could see what appeared to be a tree limb in the water. Suddenly the "limb" disappeared, almost instantly emerging again

Cases of Mistaken Identity

It is not wholly impossible that sea serpents are real beasts that have somehow eluded scientific detection. A somewhat stronger possibility is that an eyewitness may have encountered a living fossil—the remnant of a species erroneously thought to have died out millions of years ago. The most likely explanation of all is that what is described as a monster is actually a rarely seen but well-documented marine animal, such as a blue whale. Pictured below are five known animals, ancient and modern, that resemble various reported sea monsters.

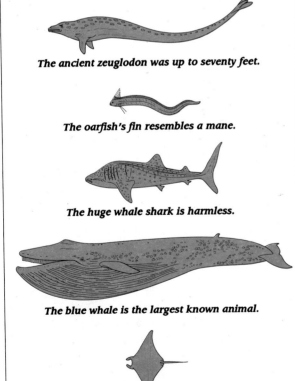

The ancient zeuglodon was up to seventy feet.

The oarfish's fin resembles a mane.

The huge whale shark is harmless.

The blue whale is the largest known animal.

The two-ton manta ray has hornlike fins.

closer to them. They realized with amazement that it was some kind of strange sea creature. Mrs. Stout later described it as having a large head, a six-foot-long neck with a floppy mane, and three humps; its only obvious body movement was the graceful lowering and raising of the neck and the swiveling of the head. The monster glided forward with swanlike smoothness and submerged and then came up "almost perpendicularly." Except for the humps, Mrs. Stout claimed, it "resembled pictures of the herbivorous, marsh-living dinosaurs."

At first, she reported, its head was turned away, as if the creature was watching the departing freighter. Then it sank once again, resurfacing even nearer the witnesses. Mrs. Stout's son became fearful and started to cry. The creature, apparently aware of the witnesses, disappeared again and next reappeared a little farther away. Mrs. Stout reassured her son, telling him the creature was obviously wary of them, as indeed it seemed to be.

LeBlond and Sibert published the results of their study in 1973. All told, twenty-three apparently legitimate first-hand accounts emerged—an impressive number, considering the limited area encompassed by the study.

n the other side of the continent, meanwhile, residents of the Chesapeake Bay area had been reporting sporadic appearances of the bay's native monster, known as Chessie, since the nineteenth century. The dark, serpentine creature began showing up quite regularly in the mid-1960s and achieved stardom of sorts in 1982, when it appeared in a three-minute videotape shot by a Marylander named Robert Frew.

On May 21 of that year, Frew and his wife, Karen, were entertaining at their Kent Island home, overlooking the bay. At around seven in the evening, the Frews and their guests spotted the monster in shallow, clear water about 200 yards from the house. The host first watched with binoculars, then grabbed his video camera and started shooting from his bedroom window. The monster headed toward a group of swimmers, continually breaking the surface of the water as it moved forward. The onlookers called out to warn the swimmers, who apparently could not hear the shouts. The creature dived and swam beneath the bathers, who did not notice it even when it appeared on the other side of them. The Frews estimated that the dark brown, hump-backed animal was thirty to thirty-five feet long and a foot in diameter. However, as it showed only part of its body each time it surfaced, it was hard to guess the exact size.

Cryptozoologists had high hopes for Robert Frew's videotape, believing that at last they would find real evidence of a sea serpent's existence, and on August 20, seven scientists affiliated with the Smithsonian Institution met to examine the footage. Herpetologist George Zug, a board member of the International Society of Cryptozoology who then chaired the institution's Department of Vertebrate Zoology, hosted the three-hour meeting. In the end, though, the tape proved inconclusive; it was blurry, and not enough of the creature was visible above the water at any one time to give a true indication of size. The tape sometimes showed an "angular structure, presumed to be the front end, but there were no eyes, ears, or mouth." Nevertheless, Zug reported, all the viewers had "a strong impression of an animate object, certainly not some kids swimming in a garbage bag"—as one underwater photographer had suggested. Unfortunately, the scientists were not able to discern what kind of animate object they were watching.

Once again, the sea serpent seemed to have eluded technology's grasp. But there remained other bits of evidence to ponder, evidence provided by the sea itself.

Over the centuries, the oceans have deposited many strange and mysterious remains on the earth's shores. Of these, perhaps none was more astonishing or controversial than the enormous carcass discovered on the rocks off the Orkney island of Stronsa (now called Stronsay) by a Scottish farmer named John Peace.

On September 26, 1808, Peace was out fishing in his boat when a large number of birds circling above the rocks caught his eye. Intrigued, he went to investigate. At first he thought that the huge lump attracting the birds was a dead

whale. But as he approached it, he discovered that it was like no whale he had ever seen. The putrefying monstrosity had several fins, or arms, and when Peace lifted the largest one with his boat hook, he found that it was surrounded by a row of ten-inch bristles.

About ten days later, the carcass washed onto the shore during a storm, and Peace and two other local men began to examine the strange remains in earnest, even measuring various parts of the body. The cartilaginous skeleton was around fifty-five feet long, with a small head, long neck and tail, bristly mane, and six "paws," each with five or six "toes." Another storm subsequently scattered the

A hulking carcass with waruslike tusks draws curious townspeople to a beach at Ataka, Egypt. Cast up by a three-day gale in the Gulf of Suez in January 1950, the creature was not positively identified by experts.

A group of onlookers maintains a prudent distance from a decomposing carcass found on a beach in Santa Cruz, California, in 1925. It appeared at first to be a monstrous animal with a thirty-foot-long neck, a huge head, and a ducklike beak, but biologists who later examined the skull concluded that it was the remains of an extremely rare beaked whale from the North Pacific.

badly decomposed carcass, but a local artist was able to draw sketches under the direction of the original witnesses.

Eventually, a description of the beast reached Patrick Neill, secretary of the Wernerian Natural History Society in Edinburgh. Neill declared without hesitation that this was the kind of creature described centuries before by the Scandinavian witness Hans Egede—a conclusion no doubt influenced by recently reported sightings of a sea serpent in the nearby Hebrides. Later, before he had even seen the witnesses's depositions or the existing bits of physical evidence, Neill proposed naming the Stronsa beast *Halsydrus* (meaning "sea water-snake") *pontoppidani.* This he did solely on the basis of a paper and some drawings by Dr. John Barclay, a fellow member of the society who had viewed some of the creature's remains in the Orkneys.

Eventually, a London surgeon and naturalist named Everard Home obtained all the information, the affidavits, and some pieces of the carcass. Home, despite a reputation marred by charges of plagiarism, was something of an expert on the huge fish known as the basking shark, and he quickly determined that the Stronsa beast was just that. Decomposition, he believed, had created the illusion of the long neck and tail, and also of the bristly mane. The six "paws" were actually four fins and two claspers, the double reproductive organs of the male shark. Home dismissed as error the creature's reported length, too great for any known basking shark, even though the men had taken careful measurements.

However correct they may have been, Home's conclusions angered the Scottish scientists, particularly John Barclay, who had embarrassed himself with his ill-informed paper on the physiology of the "sea serpent." Barclay

A huge, decomposing carcass netted by the Japanese trawler Zuiyo Maru in 1977 was photographed (below) and sketched (opposite) before the captain ordered the intriguing but nasty catch thrown overboard. The long-necked creature weighed about 4,000 pounds.

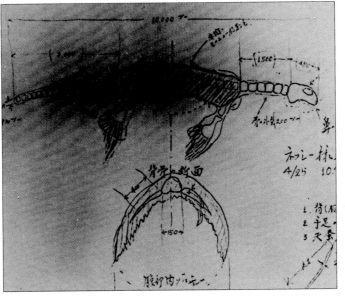

As sketched by a witness on the Zuiyo Maru, this mysterious sea creature seemed decidedly reptilian in form. But further study indicated that it was probably a basking shark.

published a reply and a counterattack—revealing even more ignorance—but Home did not deign to answer. The Scottish public, uncertain who was right, sided with Barclay, who had had the last word—if not the most correct one. The controversy continued for years, and even today some people believe that the Stronsa beast received unjust treatment and perhaps was, in fact, a sea serpent.

Most modern authorities, however, are convinced that Home was essentially correct in his identification. The cartilaginous skeleton was the key clue, since only sharks and their closest relatives have such a skeleton. All the other details fit, as well. Still, according to Bernard Heuvelmans, Home may have oversimplified the issue in dismissing the creature's length; the Stronsa beast may indeed have been an unknown giant shark.

Whatever the true identity of the Stronsa creature may be, almost all of the many other unusual strandings examined by scientists over the years have turned out to be decomposed known animals—primarily sharks, whales, or oarfish. A sea serpent has yet to appear, although the carcass held briefly by a crew of Japanese fishermen in 1977 seemed very promising.

On April 10 of that year, the *Zuiyo Maru*, a Japanese ship trawling off the coast of Christchurch, New Zealand, snared a two-ton carcass in its nets. Hauling it up from a depth of 1,000 feet, the fishermen were astonished to discover an unidentified thirty-two-foot animal with a long neck and tail and four flippers. Unfortunately for cryptozoology, the terrible stench and the fatty liquid that came oozing out onto the deck were even more impressive to the men, who feared that the animal might spoil their catch of fresh fish. And so, after taking measurements and photos, they threw the mystery beast back into the sea.

Japanese paleontologists were appalled to hear of this potentially great loss to science. Examining the photographs and also the sketches drawn by Michihiko Yano, a fishing company executive who had been on board at the time, the scientists concluded that the animal was possibly a plesiosaur, the supposedly long-extinct marine reptile that some experts believe may have survived to this day. One species is known to have lived off eastern Australia 100 million years ago.

The director general of animal research at the Japanese National Science Museum, Professor Yoshinori Imaizumi, stated that the remains were "not a fish, whale or any other mammal." In fact, he was quite positive that the beast was a reptile, and most probably a plesiosaur. "This was a precious and important discovery for human beings," Imaizumi said. "It seems to show that these animals [plesiosaurs] are not extinct after all. It's impossible for only one to have survived. There must be a group." However, as if to underscore the tantalizing nature of the search for physical evidence of the sea serpent, later examination of the data from the Japanese find indicated that the creature was in all likelihood a relatively common basking shark rather than an exotic plesiosaur.

For all the lack of ironclad physical evidence, the sheer weight of eyewitness testimony has convinced many scientists that sea serpents do exist. But even the believers are not quite sure what to make of these creatures—how to define, explain, and classify them. Theories abound, sometimes conflicting, sometimes converging.

In times past, naturalists tried to fit all sea serpents into a single zoological mold. Today, almost all investigators engaged in the search for sea serpents hold that these creatures are of several different types. The serpent seen near the yacht *Valhalla*, for example, no more resembles the San Clemente monster than an eel does a jellyfish. Neither do modern researchers believe that these animals are actually serpents. Indeed, most are probably not even reptiles; frequent use of the term *sea serpent* persists merely for the sake of tradition and convenience.

The diligent efforts of one man, Bernard Heuvelmans, have gone a long way toward unscrambling and categorizing reported marine monsters. To be sure, not every scientist—and not even every cryptozoologist, for that matter—agrees with his classifications, but most applaud his exhaustive research. Over the course of ten years, Heuvelmans collected and analyzed data on 587 occurrences that he described as "real, apparent or pretended sightings of great unknown sea-animals, serpentine in some respect." After eliminating hoaxes, errors, and vague descriptions, he found characteristics that suggested nine distinct categories of sea serpents. He called them the long-necked, the merhorse, the many-humped, the many-finned, the super-otter, the super-eel, the marine saurian, the father-of-all-the-turtles, and the yellow-belly.

Some experts, including Heuvelmans, believe that at least some types of large unidentified marine creatures are giant eels. Others suggest that the real culprit may be a zeuglodon, or primitive whale—a supposedly extinct creature whose remains figured in a notorious nineteenth-century sea-serpent hoax *(page 30)*. Still others propose that it may be a member of an unidentified, giant northern species similar to the long-necked leopard seal of the Antarctic.

One of the most persistent theories is that the sea serpent—at least the long-necked variety—is a surviving plesiosaur, as was proposed in the case of the carcass found and discarded by the Japanese fishermen. Indeed, the discovery of the coelacanth has proved that a presumably extinct creature can survive to modern times. But while the plesiosaur might look the part—it has been described as resembling "a snake that swallowed a barrel"—it could not act the part, according to most modern experts. The plesiosaur was apparently very slow, and its neck was not flexible. The vertical undulations reported by so many eyewitnesses were simply not within its capabilities; nor were the speed and agility that typify the long-necked sea serpent.

Skeptics, of course, lean toward a variety of known phenomena as explanations for sea-serpent reports. The classic porpoises-jumping-in-a-line explanation dates back to at least 1803 and continues to this day, although it would take considerable synchronization for frolicking porpoises to create the illusion of undulating coils. Large land snakes, especially pythons, are supposed to account for some sightings. But even if these snakes were large enough to pass for sea serpents and adaptable enough to survive northern climates, they would still be unable to undulate in a vertical plane, as sea monsters are said to do. Another popular explanation is that the mystery beast is really an oarfish—a monstrous-looking serpentine fish, silver in color, with bright red fins radiating out from the head and oarlike ventral fins. However, although oarfish can grow to lengths of thirty feet, their bright colors and horizontal undulations do not make them likely sea-serpent candidates. The list of known-phenomenon theories goes on and on, including even logs and seaweed.

The debate, too, seems likely to continue—between the multitude of debunkers, demanding solid physical proof, and a small but dedicated band of proponents, clinging to their intriguing fragments of evidence. "Many a man has hanged on the basis of flimsier circumstantial evidence," researchers LeBlond and Sibert wrote in defending the sea-serpent issue against the "scoffers who insist that there cannot be any more large undiscovered animals nowadays and that . . . 'sea-monsters' are the result of hallucination, error or bad faith." But the scientists conceded wryly, "We will admit that what may pass for sufficient proof in a court of law might not satisfy the criteria of incontrovertible scientific proof: the body is still missing."

Such proof will never be easy to come by: Suboceanic exploration is fraught with difficulties and danger—the seas are so vast, and humankind's boats and bathyscaphes so small. Indeed, for all our technology, the oceans and many of their inhabitants are still very nearly as enigmatic as they have ever been.

Confronting the Giant Squid

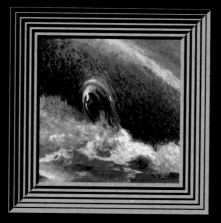

Ever since the first mariners began returning from their voyages with tales of malevolent creatures that inhabit the deep, sea monsters have lurked in the human consciousness. And one creature in particular seems to concentrate in its form the terrors of the watery world—the giant squid.

This behemoth's great cylindrical body and huge round eyes, eight snakelike arms, and pair of far-reaching tentacles have frequently been described in art and literature. Pottery from ancient Greece depicts giant squid attacking fishing boats; Japanese woodcuts show the fearsome creatures battling whales. Aristotle and Pliny both wrote of huge squid. In Norway, the beast called the Kraken seemed to combine characteristics of the giant squid with those of the octopus.

Even though sightings were frequent and the observations remarkably similar, the giant squid was still considered a mythical sea monster until the 1870s. Then, for reasons scientists were at a loss to explain, no less than a dozen of the tentacled creatures were reported in Newfoundland. Most were found stranded on the shores, and few of them were identified or examined by experts. But one chance encounter in 1873 provided three hapless fishermen and the scientific community with proof of what generations of seafarers had known all along—that the giant squid not only existed but could be a mortal threat. The harrowing story of those fishermen and their furious battle with a monster from the sea appears on the following pages.

It was just before dawn on October 26, 1873. The air was chilly and damp, and the harbor at St. John's, on the southeastern tip of the island of Newfoundland, was blanketed with fog. Two seasoned fishermen, Daniel Squires and Theophilus Piccot, dressed warmly in heavy woolen sweaters and oilskins, were setting out to net herring in a nearby cove. Piccot's twelve-year-old son, Tom, eager to learn his father's trade, joined them at the dock.

The trio settled themselves in a dory—a small, flat-bottomed boat about twenty feet long—and rowed a short distance out into Conception Bay to set their nets. Soon the fishermen noticed what they thought was a raft of seaweed. But as the boat drew nearer, they realized the large, shapeless mass was not at all what it seemed.

The object's surface was slick and purplish red in color. Although the fishermen speculated that the calmly floating form might be the body of some sea creature, apparently no one considered just then that they might be gazing at a volatile giant squid.

One of the men poked at the strange mound with a boat hook. Suddenly, the mass erupted, whipping a circular formation of eight long, thick, sucker-studded arms out of the water and through the air; exposed at their center was a long, parrotlike beak and eyes the size of dinner plates. A pair of snakelike tentacles, twice the length of the squid's arms, darted through the churning sea toward the dory. Within seconds, the giant squid had wrapped its prey in the muscular grip of a tentacle and was yanking the little boat toward its open mouth.

Wrapping a sinuous arm around the gunwale, the giant squid began pulling the small craft lower into the sea. As water rushed into their boat, the desperate fishermen flailed at the monster with their oars and bailed out water with a gallon bucket. Then young Tom Piccot snatched up a hatchet. Chopping furiously, he managed to sever the arm and tentacle that coiled around the dory; at that, the monster quickly retreated, trailing great clouds of inky fluid.

The fishermen hastily rowed for the shore, with the squid's amputated arm and tentacle still clinging to the boat. Safely back in port, the trio displayed the irrefutable evidence of their encounter. The tentacle, obviously only a portion of its total length, stretched nineteen feet; the squid's arm, unfortunately, was carried off by hungry dogs before it could be measured.

Beasts in Human Form

If tales and legends can be credited, the world of long ago was inhabited by many strange and wondrous creatures. Among the most intriguing of these beasts were the half-human, half-animal hybrids.

Many scholars have speculated about the creatures. Some believe that they sprang from the instinctive fears and anxieties of primeval people. Others maintain that as humankind began to worship animals whose strength or cunning were most feared or admired, it began to endow the animal-gods with human traits. This transfiguration was probably nurtured by attempts to picture an animal-god's exploits. A warring beast, for example, might be given human arms with which to throw a spear.

Some legends are thought to be results of encounters with unfamiliar animals or exotic peoples in far-off lands. Still others may well be only the products of fertile imaginations. Whatever their origins, human-beasts were known to cultures throughout the ancient world. A sampling of their strange and monstrous forms appears on the following pages.

A creature with the head and body of a lion, a human head, wings, and the tail of a snake appears in this Turkish bas-relief from about the tenth century BC. Probably derived from the Egyptian sphinx, the fire-breathing human-beast was said to guard the palace of the reigning monarch.

Supposedly seen as recently as 1820, the sinuous mermaid shown in this Japanese drawing is said to be a messenger from a serpent-princess who lives beneath the sea.

Legendary Denizens of the Deep

According to ancient Egyptian legend, the merman and mermaid shown in this seventeenth-century engraving once emerged from the Nile River. The amorous amphibians shared a feature considered unique among fabled fish—webbed feet.

The monk-fish and the bishop-fish, two creatures bearing a remarkable re-semblance to clergymen, were reportedly observed in Europe during the 1500s.

In a classic view of the age-old legend, a voluptuous mermaid enchants a young man in this painting from the mid-1800s. Mermaids were said to lure men with the promise of forbidden pleasures, only to devour them or hold them prisoner at the bottom of the sea.

Demi-Humans of the Land

This painting from a Greek vase of the sixth century BC depicts the warrior Theseus slaying the Minotaur. Described as the offspring of a great white bull and the unfaithful wife of Crete's King Minos, the flesh-eating monster was said to possess the body of a human and the head—and appetite—of a bull.

In ancient Egypt, the jackal-headed god called Anubis, portrayed in this bronze statue from the Ptolemaic period (332-30 BC), was thought to supervise the preparation of mummies and guard the tombs of the dead. Anubis also participated in the judgment of the deceased, weighing their hearts against the feather of truth to determine who would achieve the glory of afterlife.

The lamia of Greek mythology had the head and breasts of a human female, as shown in this seventeenth-century woodcut. The voracious creature was said to feast on men and children.

On the Andaman Islands off the coast of Burma, Marco Polo reportedly encountered a race of dog-headed men. "They are a most cruel generation," he wrote, "and eat everybody that they can catch."

The Greek satyr, a shaggy woodland spirit with the haunches of a goat, plays a rustic pipe in this seventeenth-century drawing. These merry creatures supposedly spent their time sleeping, making music, or cavorting with nymphs.

Legend has it that when the half-man, half-horse centaur Chiron was felled by a poisoned arrow, the Greek god Zeus set his image in the heavens as the constellation Sagittarius, depicted in this twelfth-century illustration.

Creatures of the Air

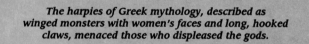

The harpies of Greek mythology, described as winged monsters with women's faces and long, hooked claws, menaced those who displeased the gods.

Wings outstretched, the figure of Maat, Egyptian goddess of truth and justice, kneels above the entrance to the tomb of Nefertari, wife of Pharaoh Ramses II.

A winged, hawk-headed man clutching a bag in his hand graces an ear ornament from ancient Peru. The figure is thought to be a courier garbed as a bird or a representation of a god.

The Greek sphinx allegedly perched outside the city of Thebes and killed passersby who failed to answer its riddles. As shown in this statue from about 570 BC, the creature had the body of a lion, the wings of an eagle, and a woman's head.

This eagle-headed genie of Assyrian legend, shown in a marble bas-relief from about 900 BC, was said to be a benevolent guardian. But tales describe evil genies who spread disharmony and inspired criminal acts.

CHAPTER 2

The Quest for Nessie

estled deep in the Scottish Highlands, surrounded by rugged mountains and forests and fields, Loch Ness is one of Europe's great lakes. Its length is a modest twenty-four miles, and its width rarely exceeds one mile; but the fantastic depth—more than 700 feet in places—makes Loch Ness by volume the third-largest body of fresh water in Europe. And it is by all odds the most mysterious. In those frigid waters, rendered dark and virtually opaque by peat leached from the land, a huge creature is said to reside.

Among the countless believers is Hugh Ayton, a farmer who in 1963 was tilling land that bordered the lake near the village of Dores. Ayton, his son Jim, and three other men were still working at 7:30 one serene August evening when the son saw something moving across the lake. The men stared where the youth was excitedly pointing. "It was big and black," said Ayton later. "The loch was calm and everything was quiet; there wasn't a noise anywhere. Just this thing moving steadily forward."

Suddenly, the men realized that they were watching "the monster" of Loch Ness lore, and in an instant, curiosity overwhelmed caution. Racing down to a nearby jetty, four of them jumped into a small rowboat equipped with an outboard motor and took off after it. "The thing was still coming down the loch," recalled Ayton, "and as we got closer, we could see more details of it. There was a long neck coming about six feet out of the water, and a head which reminded me rather of a horse, though bigger and flatter. The body was made up of three low humps—about 30 to 40 feet long in all and about four feet high. The color was dark and the skin looked rough."

The men were within about fifty yards of the creature, related Ayton, when it "rose up a little out of the water and dived and put up an enormous disturbance which swirled the boat around." A few seconds later, the head resurfaced, and then it disappeared for good. "The one feature of it that I'll always remember," said Ayton, "was the eye—an oval-shaped eye near the top of its head. I'll always remember that eye looking at us."

History does not record when the first of the lake creatures was sighted or who encountered it. Water spirits and other such beings have been a part of Highland legend for many centuries. In 565 AD, the Irish missionary Saint

Columba is said to have come across some townspeople along the River Ness burying a man who had been mauled by a monster, and the saint is supposed to have saved another swimmer from attack by what was described as "a very odd-looking beastie, something like a huge frog, only it was not a frog." The creature would have devoured the hapless soul had not the saint commanded: "Go thou no further nor touch that man. Go back at once!" The monster is said to have approached to within fifty feet of the swimmer and then sank harmlessly out of sight. Tradition notwithstanding, though, neither of these supposed incidents appears to have occurred at Loch Ness.

The early Scots called these creatures water kelpies, water horses, water bulls, or simply spirits, and mothers sternly warned their children not to play too close to the shores of lakes or rivers; the beast, or whatever it was, could take the form of a horse, galloping onto the land, enticing a child on top of its back, and then plunging with its helpless little rider back into the depths.

One of the first of the modern-day sightings is said to have occurred in 1880, when a seasoned Loch Ness waterman named Duncan McDonald was examining a boat that had sunk in the lake. McDonald was examining the wreck when he signaled frantically to be pulled to the surface. Ashen faced, trembling uncontrollably, and incoherent with fear, he was finally able to blurt out that he had seen a monster in the murky water. He had gotten a good look at one of the creature's eyes, he reported, and described it as "small, gray and baleful." According to some accounts, McDonald never entered the lake again.

Since then, there have been something like 3,000 reported sightings—from shore and from boats, in every day-light hour, some vague and some powerfully detailed—by every imaginable sort of person, singly and in groups of a score or more: farmers and priests, fishermen and lawyers, policemen and politicians, and even a Nobel prize-winning chemist, the Englishman Richard L. M. Synge, who saw the creature in 1938. Million-dollar expeditions have descended on Loch Ness. Investigators have spent months at a time scanning the lake with binoculars, have launched minisubmarines into its depths, and have probed its gloomy reaches with strobe-light cameras and sonar equipment. One investigator estimated that, for every observation, there have been 350 hours of concerted search, leading to scores of books, some scornfully debunking, others stoutly championing "Nessie," as she—for some reason, the monster seems to have been deemed female—has come to be called.

Nevertheless, the lake has yet to yield an ancient bone, a bit of tissue, or any other definitive testimony to the monster's presence. Aside from the volumes of eyewitness reports, the evidence consists of only a handful of fuzzy and ambiguous photographs and films and some debatable sonar readings. For all the ardent attention, the puzzles of Loch Ness and its elusive creature are no closer to solution now than they were that day in 1880 when Duncan McDonald was scared half to death by the ominous form he supposedly spotted in the dim, peat-stained waters.

But that is in the nature of such things. Lake monsters—immense, mysterious, menacing—are part of the folklore of many peoples in many lands. The Highlanders, not known as overly gullible or fanciful, relate that they themselves have glimpsed monsters in more than a half-dozen Scottish lakes in addition to Loch Ness. Indeed, another of the lakes,

RAFT   20 FT.

4 FT. OUT OF WATER

HUMP 8 FT.
PORTION ABOVE WATER

Loch Morar, in recent years has even shared the spotlight with Loch Ness because of the reported appearance of a monster called Morag. Monsters have also been sighted in lakes in Scandinavia, Ireland, Siberia, and Africa. And judging from eyewitness accounts, the Loch Ness beast has at least two cousins in North America. Lake Champlain, the 109-mile-long waterway between New York and Vermont and into Quebec, is home to Champ, which has been sighted more than 200 times and supposedly captured once on film. And in British Columbia, Lake Okanagan is the site of the first reported incident in which a human actually made physical contact with a lake monster.

By some accounts, the seventeenth-century French explorer Samuel de Champlain may have spotted a strange creature in the lake that bears his name. But the first recorded sighting of an unmistakably Champ-like beast did not occur until the summer of 1819, when a boatman reportedly saw a long-necked creature with its head held about fifteen feet above the water. Similar sightings followed, and toward the end of the 1800s, interest in Champ was so great that circus impresario P. T. Barnum offered a large sum for the monster, dead or alive. Nothing came of it at the time, and some observers continue to doubt that there is anything out of the ordinary living in Lake Champlain. In 1977, however, a woman on vacation in the area photographed what appears to be a head and a long neck lifting out of the lake waters *(opposite)*. And by the 1980s, the state legislatures of Vermont and New York thought it prudent—not to mention an enticement to tourism—to pass resolutions to protect Champ.

The tradition of monsters in Canadian lakes, including Okanagan, is centuries old. The Indians told of Naitaka, or snake of the water, which was part god, part demon. So strongly did they fear Naitaka that whenever they crossed the lake, they hurled in such things as live pigs and chickens to appease the ferocious monster. Not to do so was foolhardy, they thought, and there is some more-recent support for the belief. In the mid-1850s, one John MacDougall was supposedly crossing the lake with his two horses swimming behind him, attached to his canoe by ropes. Usually, MacDougall honored the Indian custom and tossed a small animal or two in the water to appease whatever malevolent creature lived there, but this time he neglected to do so. As the story goes, something unseen began to pull the horses under and would have dragged the canoe down, too, had MacDougall not whipped out his knife, cut loose the horses, and paddled for shore.

Despite such reports—or perhaps because of them—the Okanagan monster was largely dismissed as a native superstition until the 1920s, when there were repeated sightings. All of the stories indicated that the beast was harmless, and the first fears quickly turned to a curious sort of affection. Local residents gave the creature a fanciful name, Ogopogo, and by 1983, the local tourist association was offering one million dollars for proof of Ogopogo's existence. To be sure, it was a tongue-in-cheek proposition, soon dropped, that was designed to boost tourism, but the association plainly thought there was at least a slim chance of someone claiming the reward. To cover that eventuality, it took out an insurance policy with Lloyd's of London.

Not everyone was laughing, however. In 1987, a Canadian woman who wanted to be identified only as Mrs. B. Clark finally described a close encounter she had had with the monster thirteen years before. A teenager then, she was swimming toward a diving platform about a quarter of a mile offshore when "something big and heavy bumped my legs." She scrambled for the safety of the raft and watched it. "I could see a hump or coil which was eight feet long and four feet above the water, moving in a forward motion," she said. The animal was twenty-five to thirty feet long, and "kind of 'humped' itself along like a giant inchworm."

Yet for every reported sighting of a Champ or an Ogopogo, there have been a dozen of the Loch Ness monster. And so it is to Loch Ness, smaller and murkier than either Champlain or Okanagan, that dedicated monster hunters from both sides of the Atlantic Ocean have returned each summer for many decades to track their elusive quarry.

Geologists date the formation of Loch Ness to the last ice age, between 10,000 and 20,000 years ago, when a great finger of glacier gouged the lake bed out of the earth's crust. The Highland Scots have a more evocative explanation for both the loch and its name. In ancient times, goes the tale, the lake was a paradisiacal valley with a holy well, blessed by a Druid priest, whose waters cured every disease. But like most Edens, the valley lay under an omnipresent threat of destruction. The Druid had cautioned the people that each time they finished drawing water, they must immediately replace the stone that capped the well.

They obeyed the warning until one day a woman, going to the well, left her baby by the fireside in her house. No sooner had she removed the stone than she heard the child cry out. She raced back to her house and saved her child from a burning ember, but she had left the well uncovered. The waters flooded the valley. The people ran for the mountains, where their lament filled the air: *Tha loch 'nis ann!*—"There is a lake now!" Hence the name Ness.

It is easy enough to understand the belief that Loch Ness lies under an ancient curse. Set in Scotland's Great Glen, a geologic fault that splits Scotland in two from Fort William in the south to Inverness in the north, the lake is subject to strong winds that can change conditions within minutes. One moment its surface is as glassy as a mirror,

In July 1977, Sandra Mansi reportedly saw the head and neck of a strange creature rise from the waters of Lake Champlain. She quickly snapped this now-famous photograph, thought by some to reveal the lake monster known as Champ. Experts judged the photograph genuine, but since Mansi's negative was lost, skeptics have not ruled out a hoax.

Urquhart Castle, with its view of Loch Ness, would seem a good place from which to observe Nes

the lake's famous monster. Yet five centuries of castle records contain no mention of such a creature.

and the next will see it whipped into a frenzy of eight-foot waves. For centuries it has been said that Loch Ness never gives up its dead. And in truth, the temperature is so low at the bottom that bodies can be consumed by the lake's fauna before gases can form to bring a corpse to the surface.

Two deaths in the lake in this century have perpetuated its sinister reputation. In 1932, the wife of a prominent banker drowned in a boating accident; although she was an excellent swimmer and only yards from shore, her body was never recovered. Twenty years later, the noted speedboat pilot John Cobb was killed while trying to break the world water-speed record. Conditions were supposed to be ideal: A flat, breezeless calm prevailed. But Cobb's boat disintegrated when it hit an area of disturbed water at over 200 miles per hour. Some say that the turbulent patch was the monster's wake; others, though, explain that Cobb almost certainly struck the wake of his own pilot boat.

Much of Loch Ness is hidden from the winding road that runs along its southwestern shore, twisting in among the foothills and passing through bleak moorland. Even from the major road along the northern shore, the view of the water is often obscured by heavy forest. But on both shores, the road opens up at several points to reveal a stunning panorama.

The most spectacular view, where the lake is deepest and widest, is from the ruins of Urquhart Castle, once a Norman fortress that, another legend has it, was built from stones borne by witches. At one time a pawn between the conquering English and the rebellious Scots, the twelfth-century castle on Urquhart Bay now is more famous as the best place from which to spot the monster.

How a monster might have reached Loch Ness is almost as great a mystery as what the monster is. The sole waterways connecting the lake with the sea are the Caledonian Canal, first opened to navigation in 1822, and the River Ness. The canal is controlled through numerous locks that are opened only to let vessels through. The river is now too shallow to accommodate a monster-size creature, although

it would have been much deeper just after the end of the last ice age, before the land rose when relieved of the huge weight of glaciers.

Nevertheless, a creature would find a comfortable home in Loch Ness, which is rich in eels, salmon, trout, and other fish. And yet, it was not until the early 1930s that the monster seemed suddenly to burst forth after centuries of relative quiescence. The first recorded sighting of the beast came on the evening of July 22, 1930, when young Ian Milne and two companions were fishing off Tor Point, near the small village of Dores. The lads were idly casting for salmon when they were startled by a great commotion 600 yards up the loch. "I saw spray being thrown up into the air to a considerable height," reported Milne. The thing bore down on the fishermen until it was 300 yards away, then swiftly turned in a half circle and rushed away at a speed of about fifteen knots or more. "The part of it we saw would be about 20 feet long and it was standing three feet or so out of the water. The wash it created caused our boat to rock violently," said Milne, and he solemnly concluded, "It was without doubt a living creature, and I can say that it was certainly not a basking shark or a seal or a school of otters or anything normal."

Milne's account, published in the local press, stirred a mild sensation and prompted a number of letters from correspondents relating previous experiences with a supposedly similar creature. But the excitement quickly faded when no further sightings were forthcoming. Two years passed—and then in 1933, the Loch Ness monster made itself known with a vengeance. That was the year work crews repaired and resurfaced the road along the lake's north shore, and some investigators feel that there was a direct relationship between the two events. Indeed, while the commotion caused by the road builders probably was not sufficient, as some have suggested, to shake a slumbering monster from its underwater caverns, it may well be that the felling of trees along the roadway gave passersby a better view of the lake and anything on it.

Whatever the cause, on April 14, Mr. and Mrs. John

Mackay, innkeepers at Drumnadrochit, were driving along the lake when Mrs. Mackay noticed that the serene surface of the loch had been shattered by a surging, roiling mass of water. As she watched in astonishment, what seemed to be an enormous animal rolled and plunged about for almost a minute before disappearing in a great gout of foam. The Mackays related this experience to Alex Campbell, a water bailiff and also local correspondent for the *Inverness Courier.* Campbell, who would eventually claim to see the monster nearly a score of times himself, filed his story. And soon talk of the monster was rippling through the Highlands. Cynics pointed out that as managers of the Drumnadrochit Hotel, the Mackays stood to gain handsomely from the tourist draw of having a creature in the lake. In truth, Mrs. Mackay complained much later, the brewery that owned the hotel took advantage of the publicity and "sold it above our heads a couple of years later," which caused the Mackays to lose their positions.

At any rate, the monster kept popping up before the awestruck eyes of local residents and visitors alike. In one case, the thing was reportedly seen on land. On a beautiful July afternoon, George Spicer, a London businessman, and his wife were driving near the lake when suddenly a "loathsome" creature with a long neck

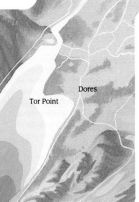

and measuring about twenty-five feet in length crossed their path. The beast appeared to be carrying a small lamb or similar animal in its mouth, Spicer said. It was, he added, "the nearest approach to a dragon or prehistoric animal that I have ever seen." In another instance in September, a party of six people said they watched from a teahouse window while the monster swam about the lake a half mile out. It seemed to have a snakelike head and neck that it pumped up and down and swung from side to side; the people saw two humps and a large tail that lashed the water. They watched in fascination for fully ten minutes before the creature moved slowly off and sank beneath the surface.

The sensation continued throughout the summer, with perhaps a score of sightings involving dozens upon dozens of people. Some eyewitnesses had nightmares for weeks. As Mrs. Spicer described the creature, "It was horrible—an abomination."

The first photograph of Nessie was taken in mid-November by a local, Hugh Gray, who had aimed his camera at a commotion in the lake 100 yards away and had snapped five pictures; four were light-struck and useless, but the fifth, though damaged, showed a vaguely defined, sinuous form in the water. Gray was hesitant to estimate the thing's size, except to say that it "was very great"; he said that the skin appeared smooth and glistening and of a dark-gray color. His negative was analyzed by several photography experts, who declared that it seemed genuine and had not been retouched.

By then the national press had picked up the story, and teams of reporters were

Loch Ness is one of three lakes that fill the Great Glen, a massive geologic fault cutting across Scotland. The largest body of fresh water in Britain, it covers nearly 14,000 acres and has an average depth of 433 feet. The loch's placid beauty belies its inhospitable nature: The water's temperature is a frigid forty-two degrees, and all but about the first few feet of water is virtually impenetrable by light.

INVERNESS

River Ness

Caledonian Canal

Dores

Tor Point

Drumnadrochit

URQUHART BAY

Urquhart Castle

Foyers

Fort Augustus

Caledonian Canal

racing north to file vivid accounts. Huge prizes were offered for the monster, dead or alive. Hotels in the area did a business such as they had never dreamed possible, and canny shopkeepers enjoyed a nice little windfall in souvenir monster pincushions, tea cozies, and chocolate effigies. Such was the crush that on holidays, cars were backed up for miles along the shore road. No less a personage than Prime Minister Sir Ramsey MacDonald was said to be so interested in the monster that he planned a special trip north in hopes of catching a glimpse.

In London, a tony seafood restaurant responded to the monster fever by offering ''Le filet de sole Loch Ness.'' And across the Atlantic in America, a woman's clothing manufacturer made quite a hit with an ensemble called ''Loch Ness,'' consisting of a dark-green frock and matching jacket with long front tails trimmed in gray fox.

As the year drew to a close, the French press, in search of relief from the grim events of the Great Depression, decided that 1933's brightest spot by far was the discovery of the monster. The Austrians, on the other hand, were decidedly unhappy, the government sourly complaining that it was all a Scottish plot to lure tourists away from the Alps and Vienna's coffee and chocolate-cake parlors.

It was an atmosphere ripe for a hoaxer, and inevitably an ingenius prank was perpetrated. In December, a self-

Hired in 1933 by the London Daily Mail to find Nessie, big-game hunter M. A. Wetherall (center) quickly discovered monster-size footprints. They were later shown to have been made by pranksters with a hippopotamus-foot umbrella stand.

head something like a snake or a huge eel. The creature was watching him, he said, and when he got to within twenty yards, it bounded swiftly away and plunged noisily into the lake. Grant made a sketch of what he had seen; the monster was about twenty feet long, with a heavy body and four limbs, the forequarters small and weak, the hindquarters massive and powerful enough that it had bounded across the road like an immense kangaroo. "It looked like a hybrid," he said.

To others, however, the creature increasingly began to look like a plesiosaur, an aquatic reptile that roamed the earth during the time of the dinosaurs, 70 million years ago.

styled big-game hunter, accompanied by a personal photographer, arrived in Loch Ness with the declared intention of bagging the monster. No sooner had the two commenced the hunt than they reported finding enormous footprints, only a few hours old, on the shore of the loch. The world waited impatiently for the British Museum's pronouncement. Finally the experts rendered their opinion: The footprints, they advised weightily, belonged to a hippopotamus. To be precise, they had been made by a stuffed hippopotamus foot, a Victorian umbrella stand belonging to a local resident with two mischievous young sons. It was never clear whether the explorers were part of the joke or the victims of it, but they quickly disappeared from the scene.

Yet while the skeptics chortled, more and more people seemed to be seeing the monster. In early 1934, there was a second land sighting. A presumably reliable young veterinary student, Arthur Grant, was motorcycling one moonlit night when he noticed a large dark object on the road ahead. Grant pulled to a stop, dismounted from his machine, and crept cautiously forward. As he approached, he reported, he could see that the object was an animal with a

As the wave of Nessie sightings continued into 1934, the publicity-minded Bertram Mills Circus of London announced it would pay £20,000 for the live monster. Some optimistic souls quickly began building cages, such as this thirty-five-ton steel model, for the beast.

The Vanishing Buru

In the farthest reaches of northeast India, in an isolated valley rimmed by the Himalayas, lies a swamp said to be inhabited by monsters. Tales of these beasts, known as burus to the Apa Tani and Dafla tribes that live in the region, have been handed down in tribal lore for generations.

In 1948, word of the legendary swamp creatures reached the ears of Ralph Izzard, a correspondent on assignment in Delhi for the London *Daily Mail.* It seemed that a British zoologist and agri-cultural officer named Charles Stonor had visited the valley, located in the province of Assam, and spoken with about thirty tribespeople who convinced him they had seen the beasts. Described as about twelve feet long, with reptilian skin and three rows of short, blunt spines that ran down its back, the four-legged buru reputedly had a long snout and clawed feet. Dark blue and white in color, the creature remained holed up in the recesses of the swamp during dry periods but came up to frolic during the rainy season, when the swamp became a lake.

Sensing both an adventure and an exclusive story for his employer, Izzard contacted Stonor, and the two arranged an expedition to Assam, under the financial sponsorship of the *Daily Mail* and the governor-general of India, Earl Mountbatten of Burma. In March 1948, with a cameraman, a battery of porters, and enough provisions for 100 days in the field, the group journeyed to the swamp.

But there was not a buru to be found. The men spent months hacking through the jungle and slogging knee-deep into the swamp, enduring constant rain and the savage bites of leeches, mosquitoes, and dim-dam flies. For hours, they stood with eyes glued to a telescope, hoping for a sign of the unusual creature. They saw some provocative shadows on the water's surface, but these proved to be only ripples caused by wind. Even the very pool in which the buru were said to live, according to Izzard, "could not have concealed as much as an otter. . . . We found it little more than three feet deep."

Although the men acknowledged defeat, they did not surrender belief. Izzard and Stonor concluded that the buru had probably lived in the valley of Assam until the neighboring tribes began cultivating the land near the swamp. Then the swamp steadily silted up, depriving the buru of its home and driving the beast to extinction before it could be found and documented.

In the Himalayas of remote northeast India, an Apa Tani tribal priest named Tamar of Hang describes the legendary swamp creature known to his people as the buru. A 1948 expedition lasting three months uncovered no trace of the reptilian beast.

The small head and serpentine neck, the immense size, the flippers and aquatic habits all seemed to fit. But that was impossible—or was it?

The reports and the growing consensus about what it might be piqued the interest of a man named Rupert Gould, the first of many who would try to identify the monster once and for all. Gould, who was thirty-seven years old when he retired from the hydrographic department of the British Admiralty in 1927, had a strong curiosity about an extraordinary range of subjects, including clockmaking, perpetual motion, the canals on Mars, Nostradamus, and the secrets of the Indian rope trick. Yet another interest was sea serpents, about which he had published a book in 1930.

s the monster reports started flooding in, Gould focused his considerable attention on Loch Ness. Arriving in Inverness in November 1933, he bought a small motorcycle that he christened Cynthia and putt-putted off to the lake. A giant of a man at a portly six foot four, Gould cut a somewhat comical figure. But he was indefatigable, cycling around the lake and conducting interviews with about fifty people who had allegedly seen the monster. In 1934, without ever having sighted the monster himself, he published *The Loch Ness Monster and Others,* the first book on the subject. The Loch Ness monster, Gould said, was a descendant of his old friend, the sea serpent.

Having delivered his verdict, Gould lost interest in the monster and went on to his next starring role, in the popular British Broadcasting Corporation's "Brains Trust" program. His book impressed few zoologists, but it captured the imagination of Sir Edward Mountain, an insurance company millionaire who had come to the Highlands to fish for salmon. In the summer of 1934, Sir Edward personally financed the first monster expedition at Loch Ness.

Its members were twenty local men whom Sir Edward had recruited from the unemployment rolls. Scottish to the core, they solemnly entered their occupations as Watchers for the Monster on their state welfare cards. Sir Edward equipped his team with box cameras and binoculars and posted the men at various points around the lake for five weeks, nine hours a day. The monster watchers reported numerous sightings and took twenty-one photographs. But while King George V expressed interest in the hunt and some members of the royal family visited the lake, nothing conclusive emerged from Mountain's ambitious hunt. Mountain himself, after studying the prints produced by his minions, speculated that the monster might in fact be a gray seal that had come up the River Ness in pursuit of salmon, found its way into the lake, and was then unable to get out. Zoologists who viewed a film made later by James Fraser—who headed the Mountain expedition—tended to agree, although some of them held that the beast was a whale or even a large otter.

There was one photograph of the monster, however, that could not be dismissed quite so lightly by the zoologists—or anyone else, for that matter. Earlier, in April, a London surgeon named Robert Kenneth Wilson, on vacation in the Highlands, took four snapshots of something causing what he termed "a considerable commotion" in Loch Ness. When they were developed, two exposures were blank. But the third clearly and dramatically showed what seemed to be an animal's upraised head and neck, and the fourth showed the head disappearing into the water.

Decades later, the third photograph—often called the Surgeon's Photograph—remains the most famous documentation of Nessie. It is also the most controversial. Skeptics sometimes claim that Wilson took the photograph on April Fool's Day—although others maintain that it was in fact taken April 19. Moreover, it is said that Wilson told a close friend he had faked the picture. But Wilson's widow, queried on the matter years afterward, staunchly asserted that it was genuine.

As World War II engulfed Europe, the Loch Ness monster was largely forgotten. And when sightings were reported occasionally during the late 1940s and 1950s, not many people took them seriously; it was as though the furor of the 1930s had exhausted the public's capacity for excitement

about such things. In 1947, for example, an Inverness bank manager named J. C. Forbes said that he had seen the creature, and a local newspaper soon featured a scornful letter:

Dear Sir,

Although not acquainted with Mr. J. C. Forbes, Manager of the National Bank, Inverness, I should like to confirm his statement. From my viewpoint in the loch I could see Mr. Forbes distinctly on the shore with his friends and I actually saw them leap to safety when I came racing up the loch.

Might I please ask sightseers to return their empty whisky bottles, for the amount of broken glass in and around the loch is very dangerous to us amphibians.

Yours faithfully,

The Loch Ness Monster

During this time, the only person to pursue the monster seriously was Constance Whyte, a housewife who had grown familiar with Loch Ness when her husband became manager of the Caledonian Canal. She never saw the monster herself, but she spent two decades collecting and evaluating scores of eyewitness impressions.

In 1957, she published a book, *More Than a Legend,* which became required reading for all future monster hunters. For one thing, Whyte put together the most meticulous analysis yet of what had been seen in the lake. For another, she suggested that the lake, rather than containing a solitary monster, might hold a family of prehistoric creatures that had been trapped there since the last ice age.

Yet it remained for a young Englishman named Tim Dinsdale to rekindle international interest in Loch Ness. Be-

fore and since his involvement, there have been people who have championed Nessie. Dinsdale alone, however, devoted his life to establishing the monster's existence.

One evening in 1959, Dinsdale, then a thirty-four-year-old aeronautical engineer, was spending a comfortable evening in his home in the south of England when he opened a favorite magazine to an article about the Loch Ness monster. He had heard of the monster, of course, and was mildly curious about it. But as he read, he "became aware of a growing interest," he later recalled in *Loch Ness Monster,* one of three books the engineer would write on the subject. That night Dinsdale slept fitfully, dreaming that he walked the lake's steep shores and peered into its inky depths in hopes of finding the monster. When he awoke, he realized that he had found his life's mission.

For the next year, Dinsdale painstakingly analyzed all the available data. Then in April 1960, he set out on what was to be the first of many 600-mile journeys from his home to Loch Ness. Although he would make the trip again more than fifty times and spend countless months on the water and observing from the shore, this brief visit was to prove his most successful.

Dinsdale pursued the monster for six days. Rising near dawn, he watched the lake through binoculars from various points on shore. Each time he drove from one point to the next, he prepared for a sudden sighting by setting up his movie camera, equipped with a telephoto lens, on a tripod next to the driver's seat. When not keeping watch, he interviewed people who claimed to have seen the creature.

After five days, Dinsdale was almost ready to give up. But he decided to stay one more day. Again rising at dawn, he watched the lake for nearly four hours without success and was hungrily heading back to his hotel for breakfast when he took a few minutes to set up the camera in his car.

He was coasting down a hill when something in the lake caught his eye. Stopping abruptly, he snatched up his binoculars and peered intently at a long oval shape, mahogany colored, in the water. Then it began to move. Dinsdale dropped his binoculars and started the camera.

He filmed the monster for four minutes as it swam west on a zigzag course at distances of from 1,300 to 1,800 yards. Then he took a gamble. Hoping to get close enough to see the monster's head and neck, he raced for the water's edge—only to find that the object had disappeared.

The importance of Dinsdale's film would not be fully appreciated for almost six years. In late 1965, at the request of a member of Parliament, David James, himself a Loch Ness monster hunter, of the Joint Air Reconnaissance Intelligence Centre, part of Britain's Royal Air Force, agreed to analyze the film. JARIC estimated that the object was at least six feet wide and five feet high. Most significantly, JARIC concluded that it was neither a surface boat nor a submarine, and therefore "probably an animate object."

Dinsdale, for his part, did not wait for official encouragement. He returned to the lake for nine days in July 1960, for ten chilly days in March 1961, and again in May. In fact, from 1960 until his death in late 1987, he would average two visits to Loch Ness each year. Often, he stayed for the entire summer, living and sleeping on his sixteen-foot cabin cruiser, *Water Horse,* for weeks at a time.

Extended absences from his family were not the only occupational penalty of monster watching. Dinsdale also endured a bout of pneumonia, tumbled painfully down precipitous slopes, and weathered stormy nights when it seemed that neither *Water Horse* nor he would survive the wind and waves. But in all those years, Dinsdale had only two more tantalizing glimpses of the beastie, the name he borrowed from the local residents.

For much of that time, however, Dinsdale had plenty of company at Loch Ness. His film inspired a host of new expeditions, from individual ventures to impressively organized armies of volunteers. The largest and longest-lived effort was the Loch Ness Phenomena Investigation

From her home near Urquhart Bay, Winifred Cary has witnessed numerous efforts to prove that the Loch Ness monster exists. Cary needs no further evidence; she claims to have seen the elusive beastie fifteen times.

In 1958, trout farmer H. L. Cockrell photographed what some believe to be Nessie moving through the loch at dawn. Others contend the object is a floating log.

London surgeon R. Kenneth Wilson's 1934 image of a head and neck coming from the loch might be a monster; skeptics see an otter or diving bird.

Lachlan Stuart said he photographed a three-humped beast in 1951; some call the picture a hoax.

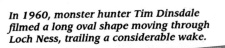

In 1960, monster hunter Tim Dinsdale filmed a long oval shape moving through Loch Ness, trailing a considerable wake.

This 1934 image by F. C. Adams seems to reveal a fin emerging from the foam, but the shot's poor quality makes analysis difficult.

Controversy surrounds this P. A. MacNab photograph from Urquhart Bay. Some say it only shows the wakes of trawlers in the loch.

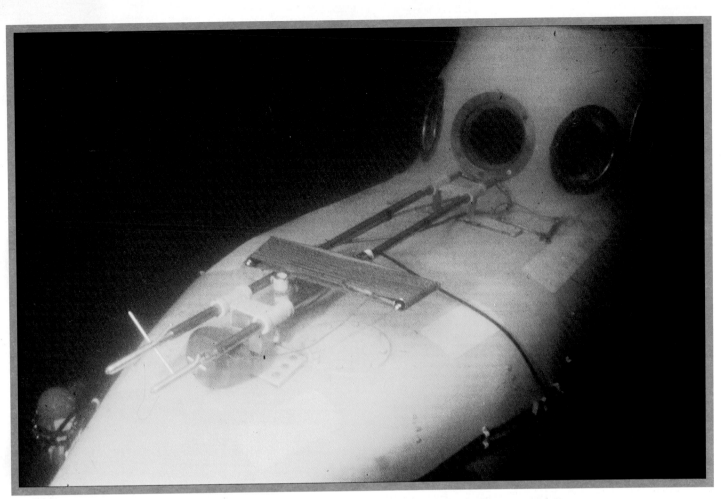

In August 1969, a one-person submarine called Viperfish was fitted with sonar equipment and biopsy harpoons intended to withdraw tissue samples from its targets. After the submarine made several problem-plagued dives into Loch Ness, the project was abandoned.

Bureau, later shortened to Loch Ness Investigation, or LNI.

Its driving force was David James, the M.P. who was best known at that time for two daredevil escape attempts, the second of which was successful, from a German prison camp during World War II. In 1962, James organized the LNI with Constance Whyte, naturalists Sir Peter Scott (son of the famous Antarctic explorer Robert Scott) and Richard Fitter, and Norman Collins, deputy chairman of a British television production company.

Later that year, in what would be the first of many expeditions on the loch, James and two dozen volunteers scanned the lake with binoculars and cameras by day. By night, they beamed army searchlights on the inky waters. As often as not, what they illuminated were other monster hunters, for the lake was becoming positively crowded.

Lt. Col. H. G. Hasler, who had led the famous "Cockleshell Heroes" canoe raid against German warships during World War II, had arrived earlier to patrol the lake in his sailboat, scanning the surface and listening through hydrophones for underwater noises. Student volunteers in a Cambridge expedition mounted shore cameras and explored the lake's depths with sonar.

The 1962 assault on Loch Ness produced some scraps of evidence that were compelling only to the already converted. In subsequent years, the LNI, using battalions of volunteers, maintained a round-the-clock camera watch on about 70 percent of the lake from May to October. By James's count, they devoted no fewer than 30,000 work-hours to scrutinizing the surface of the lake and still more time collecting the accounts of eyewitnesses. They also pursued the monster with sonar, hovered over the lake in helicopters, and put out pebbles soaked in salmon oil and foul-smelling substances they hoped would act as a sex lure. They piped Beethoven's Sixth Symphony underwater. They recorded noises from the deep and played them back.

In 1969, the LNI deployed a midget submarine named *Viperfish* in order to plumb the depths and—it was hoped—fire biopsy harpoons into the monster to collect tissue samples. On its first dive, the bright-yellow submarine buried its nose in the silt at the bottom and had to blow ballast to extricate itself. Even the most dedicated researchers reluctantly conceded that the submarine was too noisy, too slow and unwieldy to catch up with Nessie.

For several of the LNI's summers at Loch Ness, the monster hunt was largely directed by Roy Mackal, the first member of the scientific establishment to take the creature seriously. In 1965, Mackal was a forty-year-old biochemist from the University of Chicago who had won renown for his research on deoxyribonucleic acid, or DNA. He was on vacation in London and feeling the need to escape the bustle of big-city life when he came across a travel poster advertising the Scottish Highlands. A few days later, he was overlooking Loch Ness from the shore at Urquhart Bay and noticed one of the LNI's observation vans. He was fascinated.

Before he returned to Chicago, Mackal had met with David James at his estate on the Isle of Mull and viewed Dinsdale's film in London. His mind was made up; Mackal became a Loch Ness monster hunter and the LNI's point man in America, raising the first substantial money for the investigation and securing its first real hearing among members of the scientific community. During the summers he made the pilgrimage to Loch Ness. But it was not until 1970 that Mackal himself actually saw the monster.

He was retrieving hydrophones that had been set out to record underwater sounds when, out of the corner of his eye, he saw the water roil. A rubbery-looking triangular object popped out about a foot from the surface and then disappeared, to be followed by what seemed to be the smooth-skinned back of an animal of some kind. After a minute or so the thing vanished without a trace. Having seen the beast to his own satisfaction, Mackal continued to take an interest in the pursuits of the LNI team, but he also felt free to turn his attention to other elusive beasts, including Ogopogo and Champ. In 1980, he embarked on a search in the Congo for the Mokele-mbembe, a supposed sauropod dinosaur (*pages 91-97*).

By the time Mackal began branching out from the search for the Loch Ness monster, however, another American who would prove critical to the quest had become deeply involved. He was Robert Rines, a Boston patent lawyer who was forty-eight years old in 1970 when he heard Mackal speak about monster hunting at a conference Rines attended at the Massachusetts Institute of Technology, his alma mater. Something of a maverick, Rines had originally taken his degree in physics but then had embarked on a successful legal career while obtaining patents of his own for inventions in sonar and radar. He helped to establish a New Hampshire law school dedicated to turning out entrepreneurial-minded patent lawyers who would lead inventors through the jungle of government red tape.

In 1963, Rines and a few wealthy friends had founded an organization called the Academy of Applied Science, to support unusual areas of research. The academy had no official university affiliation or established research program, but it did include some individuals with impres-

Biochemist Roy Mackal takes mock aim with a crossbow armed with the biopsy harpoon he designed in hopes of identifying the Loch Ness monster through analysis of tissue samples. The dartlike instrument could also be mounted on a submarine (opposite). The idea of taking such action against Nessie outraged locals and provoked a debate in the House of Lords, but Mackal's harpoons never found their mark.

sive scientific credentials. And many of its interests coincided with those of the Loch Ness monster hunters.

Rines arrived at the lake in 1970. He brought along Martin Klein, a fellow MIT graduate who had invented an extremely sensitive type of side-scan sonar used in searching for sunken ships and in offshore oil drilling. Rines was immediately encouraged; Klein's invention indicated the presence of large moving objects, ten to fifty times larger than the biggest fish known to inhabit Loch Ness. It also suggested the existence of underwater caverns in which the monster might lurk.

The next year, Rines came equipped with an underwater camera synchronized to a powerful strobe light. It had been loaned to him by Harold "Doc" Edgerton, an MIT professor who had invented the strobe light and developed time-lapse photography; for years, Edgerton had been the lighting expert for Jacques Cousteau, the undersea explorer, and was known to Cousteau's crew as Papa Flash. Two years passed without event, and then in 1972, Rines was finally rewarded with photographs that were to be among the most important and hotly debated exhibits in the case for the Loch Ness monster.

In the very early hours of an August day, sonar equipment on the LNI boat, *Narwhal*, picked up the presence of a large, submerged object. Minutes later, salmon began frantically leaping about the water's surface, evidently trying to escape some sort of predator. Suspended at a depth of about forty-five feet, the Edgerton camera captured an extraordinary image. The photograph, enhanced by computer at the California Institute of Technology's Jet Propulsion Laboratories, showed what many saw as a large flipperlike limb of an unseen creature. Estimates placed the flipper's length at about eight feet and its width at about four feet. Three years later, Rines was to produce more dramatic evidence.

On a June day in 1975, his underwater cameras were triggered by two sonar returns about six hours apart. For some reason, Rines did not have the film developed immediately. Two months passed before he got around to dropping off the 2,000-picture roll at the laboratory of a friend, Charles Wyckoff, a photographic genius who had developed the high-speed film used to photograph atom-bomb tests. But then Rines and Wyckoff were astounded.

The first of the sonar-activated photographs seemed to show the long, curving neck, bulbous torso, and front flippers of a huge animal. At the end of the long neck, part of which was eclipsed in shadow, was the suggestion of a small head. Wyckoff calculated that the portion of the animal shown must have been about twenty feet long—and the body of the beast extended beyond the frame. More amazing still was the second image; it was a close-up of a grotesquely wrinkled object. Were investigators finally looking at the gnarled face of the Loch Ness monster? They thought so. The Gargoyle Photograph, as it became known, showed what appeared to be two small eyes and two horn-like protuberances, their bilateral symmetry characteristic of a living creature. Wyckoff estimated that the head was two feet long.

The photographs provoked a furor that was unprecedented, even by the standards of Loch Ness. For the first time, the scientific community seemed prepared at least to consider the possibility of a creature in the lake and to speculate about its identity.

Dr. George R. Zug, curator of reptiles and amphibians at the Smithsonian Institution's National Museum of Natural History in Washington, D.C., said he was convinced that

Encouraged by sonar readings he had picked up at Loch Ness, Robert Rines rigged an underwater camera and strobe flash to the sonar equipment and anchored it on a shelf in Urquhart Bay. Any movements within sonar range were automatically recorded on a graph (left) and on film. In August 1972, Rines's apparatus detected a provocative image thought to be a large fin or flipper (below). While some critics discount this photograph, other investigators believe it proves that enormous unidentified creatures live in the murky depths of the lake.

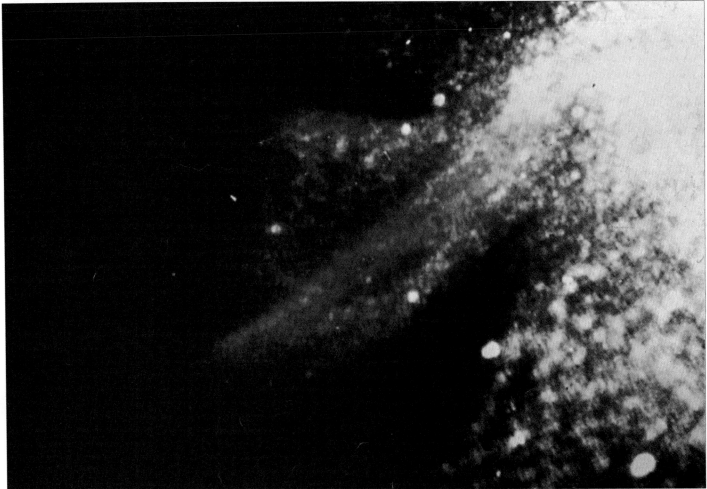

there was a population of large animals in the lake; it was obviously impossible for a single beast to have survived since the Ice Age. Sir Peter Scott, who had been inspired by the 1972 flipper photograph to paint an artist's impression of two Nessies and exhibit them in London with his celebrated wildfowl paintings, urged the Royal Society of Edinburgh and associated universities to sponsor a Loch Ness monster symposium to review the photographs. To the monster hunters' delight, such a conclave was indeed scheduled.

But no sooner had the monster hunters won some respect than their credibility collapsed. Word of the photographs was leaked to the press, which promptly ran the news under screaming headlines. Then, scientists at the British Museum, whom David James had asked to examine the photographs, issued their verdict. The response dealt a body blow to the monster hunters' hopes of a hearing.

None of the photographs proved that an animal existed in Loch Ness, the scientists said. Instead, they theorized that the image of a body and neck might actually be caused by small gas bubbles in the air sacs of the larvae of phantom midges, tiny, mosquito-like insects often found in Scottish lochs. As for the gargoyle head, they said that it could be a dead horse or even a tree. The year-end conference in Edinburgh was abruptly canceled.

Worse, there were now suggestions that the

Robert Rines inspects an underwater camera used during his search for Nessie. Once activated by sonar, the shutter clicked at regular intervals until the object being tracked strayed out of range.

photographers were perpetrating a hoax. Sir Peter Scott had dubbed the monster *Nessiteras rhombopteryx,* Greek for "the Ness marvel with the diamond-shaped fin." Wags pointed out that the phrase could be read as an anagram for "Monster hoax by Sir Peter S." Rines countered sharply with an anagram of his own, "Yes, both pix are monsters. R."

The scorn was the most intensive since the great hippopotamus-print fraud of 1933. Yet all along, anyone offering evidence that the beast existed had had to deal with a coterie of doubters determined to prove that it absolutely did not.

The first of the naysayers to publish his views had been Maurice Burton, formerly of the British Museum and a respected zoologist. At one time he had also been a firm believer in the monster. In fact, Dinsdale had borrowed one of Burton's cameras to take with him on his first trip to the loch in 1960. Dinsdale, of course, had his famous sighting and had gone on to become a celebrity, while Burton remained in the shadows. That fact, it has been suggested, may have influenced Burton's reversal of opinion.

At any event, in a 1961 book titled *The Elusive Monster,* the zoologist ventured that many of the monster sightings were probably of otters, fish-eating aquatic members of the weasel family that are known to inhabit the lake in some numbers. Otters are large, measuring almost six feet at times. They have small heads,

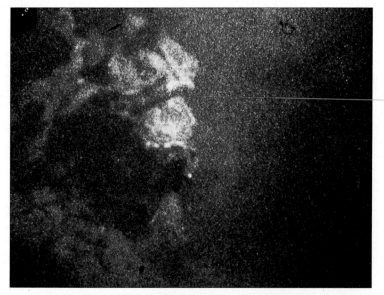

To some viewers, Robert Rines's famous 1975 photograph reveals the Loch Ness monster's horned head; more recent evidence indicates, however, that the object may be a tree stump.

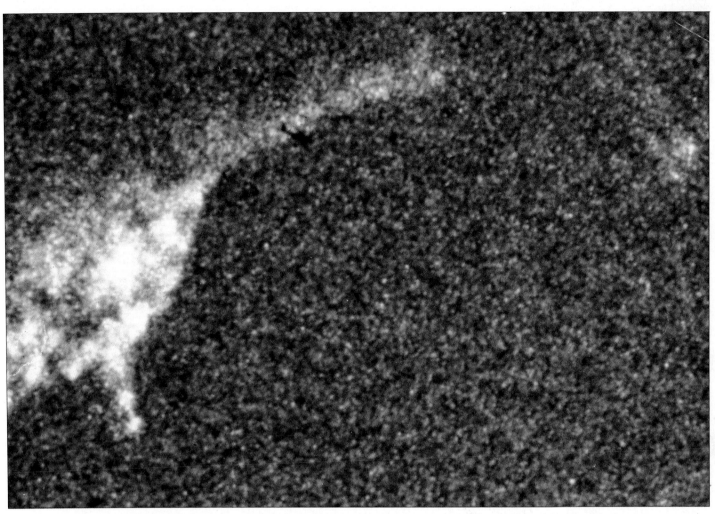

This 1975 photograph by Rines may depict the head and body of a lake monster—or gas bubbles rising from the bottom.

long sinuous necks, and prominent tails, the whole covered with a smooth, dark fur that glistens when wet. And, according to Burton, they are highly elusive. "An otter may work a river near a village and nobody be aware of its presence," he stated. "It needs a pack of hounds to give any certainty of bringing one to view." But the size? Illusion and delusion, said Burton. An alarmed or curious otter might stretch its already-substantial neck until it appeared to rise at least four feet out of the water—particularly to an impressionable observer, who might then estimate the whole creature to be twenty to twenty-five feet in length. "Most people who have claimed to have seen this animal," continued Burton, "give evidence at the same time of having experienced shock, surprise or even terror. At such moments we tend to see things bigger than they are."

All things considered, then, it appeared that the famous Surgeon's Photograph of 1934 could well be that of an alarmed otter; Dr. Wilson had merely captured the head and neck of one of the animals. Other observers who claimed to have seen the monster, Burton continued, had been fooled by such things as boats, birds, and swimming deer, seen at a distance and distorted by mirages.

As for Dinsdale, Burton said, he had actually filmed a local fishing boat; the humps on the monster's back were consistent with "a row of sou'westers worn by several men sitting from stem to stern in a fifteen-foot dinghy—no uncommon sight on Loch Ness." But there Burton may have been on shaky ground, since most of the loch's fishermen went out alone or in pairs.

Burton argued that what really accounted for many of the sightings were large mats of rotting vegetable matter such as leaves, branches, and other debris. When these mats decompose and rise from the bottom, he said, they release bubbles of gas that cause currents on the surface.

The trouble with this theory is that such gas bubbles apparently do not occur on Loch Ness. According to Ronald Binns, another skeptic who set out to debunk the Loch Ness monster in his 1983 book, *The Loch Ness Mystery Solved,* humic acids in the lake prevent rapid putrefaction. As a result, vegetable matter sinking to the floor of the lake crumbles to powder, and no gas is generated. Similarly, Binns dismissed another theory that the monster sightings are simply water-logged pine trees propelled by gases.

But Binns did agree with Burton that many of the so-called monsters glimpsed in the lake were actually mirages or otters, birds, deer, and other conventional animals. He added that Dinsdale had been overexcited and subsisting on a few hours' sleep each night for a week during his April 1960 visit and had thus unwittingly filmed a motorboat.

All of the important Rines photographs as well as the sonar findings continued to come under heavy criticism. In 1983 two American engineers, Alan Kielar and Rikki Razdan, borrowed the academy's raft on Loch Ness to set up 144 sonar devices over the surface. Any object more than ten feet long that passed beneath them would set off an alarm, and the sonar would track it automatically.

After several months they returned home empty-handed. When they reviewed the academy's earlier data on Nessie, they concluded that many of the sonar contacts had been caused by boats or stationary objects and that some of the data contained mathematical errors. The engineers also reported with raised eyebrows that a local woman had helped locate the monster for Rines by dowsing. But all of that was trivial compared with their next

announcement—concerning the 1972 flipper photograph.

In view of their suspicions, the two engineers had asked the laboratory that carried out the computer enhancement, a process it had performed for closeup photographs of planets taken by space probes, to send them copies of the enhanced flipper photograph. What they received was grainy and indistinct, in marked contrast to the published photograph. News stories about their findings seemed to accuse Rines of retouching. Rines retorted that he had combined various enhancements to come up with the flipper image. That was a standard procedure, he said, and the laboratory backed him up. But the accusation nevertheless tarnished the most convincing piece of evidence that Nessie did in fact exist.

Sir Peter Scott based his 1973 painting Courtship in Loch Ness on Robert Rines's flipper photograph (page 79). Scott's creatures resemble plesiosaurs—presumably extinct reptiles that seem to fit some descriptions of Nessie.

And there has been further criticism of the classic Surgeon's Photograph. A Scottish architect named Steuart Campbell, who has made a thorough study of the evidence concerning Nessie, asserts that the Wilson photograph is an out-and-out hoax. Given the angle at which the camera had to be held and the lack of foreground in the picture, Campbell calculated, Wilson had to have stood about 200 feet from the object he photographed, rather than the 600-plus feet he had reported to Constance Whyte. By exaggerating about his distance from the object, Campbell said, Wilson was trying to pass off an otter as the monster. Yet another analysis, however, by two University of British Columbia oceanographers, purports to show that Wilson's controversial photograph does indeed indicate a large creature whose neck is protruding about four feet above water level.

In seeking to discredit the monster sightings, skeptics have found ammunition in the numbers of outright hoaxers and poseurs who have been involved in the Loch Ness controversy. Of them all, the most outrageous may have been Frank Searle, a self-styled "monster-hunter extraordinary," who was the bane of ordinary monster hunters for a number of years.

A former British army paratrooper, Searle was a manager for a London fruit company when he set up a makeshift tent on a farm near Loch Ness in June 1969. The LNI accepted him at first as another devoted monster hunter, even lending him a movie camera for his pursuit. During the next three years he claimed several sightings but did not

have any photographs to show for his pains. Then his luck abruptly changed.

In July 1972, Frank Searle produced a photograph that other investigators hailed; it showed a large hump in a swirl of water. A few months afterward, he offered three more pictures—of a series of humps, a neck, and a large head—that he took, he said, when the creature suddenly appeared beside his dinghy, dived, and reappeared on the other side. Before long, Searle was putting together a thick scrapbook of Nessie cameos and attracting international attention. However, he was also becoming something of an embarrassment for his egregious hucksterism.

From the "Loch Ness Information Center," a hut next to his new trailer home, he sold postcards of some of his pictures as well as an audio-cassette of his version of the Loch Ness story. He published a book, *Nessie: Seven Years in Search of the Monster,* in which he grumbled about his lack of official recognition; reviled the efforts of the LNI, Rines, and Dinsdale; and boasted of the young female "Loch Ness groupies" from abroad with whom he had shared his trailer.

s the years progressed, Searle lost whatever credibility he had once enjoyed among Loch Ness investigators. Skeptics hooted that he never had a fellow witness to the two-dozen sightings he claimed. Those who scrutinized his snapshots thought that some of the "monsters" were nothing more than out-of-focus floating branches or trees. At one point, Steuart Campbell accused Searle of actually faking photographs, clumsily superimposing a picture of a reptile on a picture of the lake.

Yet Searle continued to attract naive tourists and other gullible types, until finally, at the end of 1983, he sent out his last newsletter from Loch Ness, in which he announced that he was leaving the lake in order to hunt for buried treasure. Ironically, he had outlasted many of the genuine researchers. And, inadvertently, the controversy over his snapshots highlighted one critical aspect of the monster hunt: the difficulty of obtaining authentic photographs, a problem that has been characterized by people like Dinsdale as the Loch Ness hoodoo.

For photographers, the monster is the most frustrating of subjects. The creature surfaces so quickly that even veteran investigators are caught unprepared and stare amazed until it submerges. Sometimes it seems to materialize only as a flicker in the corner of one's eye. Surprisingly often, the apparatus itself malfunctions, or a crucial photographic plate is somehow lost or broken. Because of this apparent ill fortune and the creature's elusiveness, some imaginative researchers have suggested that Nessie is not a flesh-and-blood monster at all but some sort of psychic phenomenon.

And indeed, Loch Ness has seen its share of the oc-

cult. Legend tells of a ghost ship, perhaps the one in which Saint Columba traveled the loch more than 1,400 years ago, that appears to someone every 20 years, sailing through the nighttime waters, bluish and magical, with billowing sails on its single mast and ropes neatly coiled on deck. It was reportedly seen in 1922, 1942, and 1962; so far, though, no one has come forward to describe a 1982 visit. In the early 1900s, Aleister Crowley, a well-known English practitioner of black magic, bought a house near the lake, declared himself a laird, and supposedly summoned up such demons that his lodge keeper went mad and tried to kill his wife and children; there were rumors of human sacrifices, and to this day the local folk avoid the place in fear.

An ambience of eeriness seems to envelop the monster itself. Some feel that the presence is malevolent, so much so that in 1973, the Rev. Dr. Donald Omand performed an exorcism of the evil atmosphere he felt in the area; he failed to exorcise the creature and came away convinced that it caused "mental instability" in those who pursued it. Dedicated monster hunters vigorously argue that point, though they confess to feelings of acute anxiety now and again. Over the years, many of them have fallen ill during their search. Tim Dinsdale, for one, sometimes experienced such sharp feelings of unease at several locations along the shore that he wondered whether a violent history had left a permanent "residue of evil" at these places.

Yet while Dinsdale did not dismiss the otherworldly aspects of the Loch Ness monster, he—like most of his colleagues—persisted in the belief that there is some rational explanation for all the many sightings over so many years. One of the most popular and appealing theories continues to be that the creature is a plesiosaur, one of a small remnant population that somehow survived the last ice age and adjusted to life in Loch Ness.

Proponents of the plesiosaur theory point to the capture in 1938 of a coelacanth, the huge prehistoric fish that was believed to have met the plesiosaur's fate. Nor is the plesiosaur the only ancient creature that has been nominated for Loch Ness. Indeed, it has even been suggested that

Nessie is an elongated version of a prehistoric worm. One longtime monster watcher, a former marine engineer named F. W. Holiday, has argued that the monster is a giant aquatic worm previously found only in fossil remains—and at a maximum length of fourteen inches. But he has little company in that view. Critics point out that the worm could never match the monster in diameter. Only a few of the invertebrates, such as the giant squid and the octopus, are large enough to approach the monster in size, and they do not resemble it in any other respect.

Many investigators, including Adrian Shine, an energetic London salesman and amateur naturalist who began working with the LNI in the summer of 1973, think that a species of fish, or perhaps a species of eel, is the most sensible answer to the mystery of Loch Ness. The loch is rich in salmon and eels, both of which can grow to considerable lengths. Furthermore, they can travel swiftly and would rarely surface. But opponents of that theory note that fish could not change depth levels at the rates established by sonar tracking. Eels undulate from side to side, while the Loch Ness monster reportedly undulates from top to bottom. And if the monster were a fish, they say, what would account for the land sightings?

That reduces the field of known creatures to mammals. A likely contender, in the view of some scientists, is one of the orders of mammals, such as seals, whales, or sea cows, that are monster-size and capable of surviving for long periods in fresh water. Mackal, after considering candidates ranging from a large sea slug to a giant, newtlike amphibian, finally seems to have settled on the zeuglodon, a long, serpentine, primitive whale thought to have been extinct for 20 million years.

Exceptionally long-necked seals and otters remain the favorite candidates of those bent on explaining the monster in conventional terms. But believers in Nessie as a wholly unconventional creature continue to argue, as did Sir Edward Mountain as far back as 1934, that seals tend to be sociable, frolicking in the water and loping onto land. Otters may indeed be of a more fugitive nature, but they are not so

aquatic that they could live and breed in the water as the monster presumably does. Nor can they dive to the 700-foot levels where sonar has detected moving objects.

If the identity of the monster is a mystery, its numbers are an even greater puzzle. Both monster hunters and skeptics generally speak of a single creature, but two or three of the creatures have sometimes been reported together, and it is widely agreed that a solitary animal could not survive for centuries in the lake. Based on the size of the lake and its food supply, George Zug of the Smithsonian has estimated that the number of Nessie-like creatures in the loch could range from 10 to 20 individuals, if they weigh about 3,000 pounds each, to as many as 150 animals weighing 330 pounds each.

While others carry on that debate, the hunters want nothing more than to establish that Nessie exists. And so year after year, Rines and his academy, along with other investigators, have returned to the lake in hopes of putting that single all-important question to rest. But since 1975, nothing has been as impressive as the Rines photographs.

It was on the strength of those photographs that the academy returned to Loch Ness in 1976, with the financial support of the *New York Times,* to stage the most ambitious and technologically sophisticated investigation yet. Rines assembled a team of more than two dozen highly regarded scientists, including Edgerton and Wyckoff, from the United States, Canada, and Britain. The expedition arrived with 2,000 pounds of gear, and in June, deployed a veritable arsenal of sonar devices and photographic equipment. The imaging apparatus included a time-lapse, strobe-triggered 16-mm camera set to take a picture every fifteen seconds; a pair of 35-mm stereo cameras mated to the most powerful strobe light yet used at Loch Ness; and a television camera that would operate round-the-clock and produce a video record of everything that passed before its lens.

The array was suspended 40 feet below a raft moored in 120 feet of water about 100 yards offshore from Temple Pier, near Castle Urquhart. Power lines and a television ca-

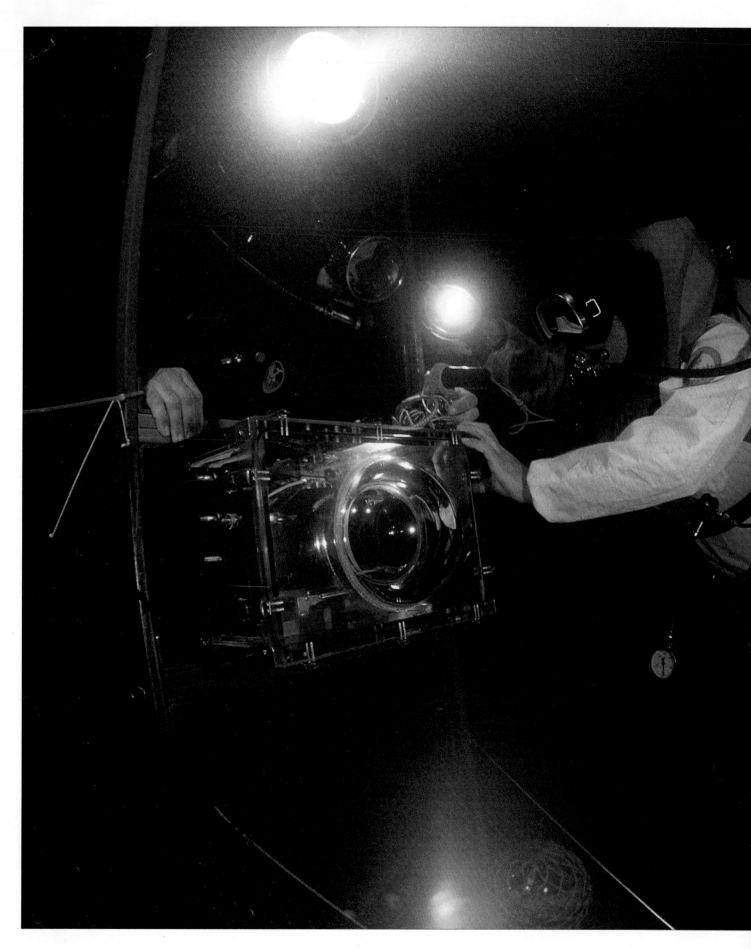

Members of an underwater expedition set up a sonar-controlled camera in the murky waters of Urquhart Bay. Dispatched to Loch Ness in 1976 by National Geographic magazine, this team tried to lure Nessie toward the lens by displaying lights to catch the creature's eye, and by broadcasting sounds of distressed fish and putting bait in the water to whet its appetite—all to no avail.

ble led to a control room in a small cottage on shore. By means of the television, relays of scientists would monitor the time-lapse camera popping away every fifteen seconds—and be prepared to punch in the high-powered strobes for the 35-mm stereo cameras the instant they saw anything suspicious.

For two months, the expedition members studied the television monitor and scanned the waters of the lake with their sonar. They returned home without clear proof one way or the other. In an exceptionally hot, dry summer, temperatures at the upper water levels of the lake had climbed fifteen degrees from their normal forty-two degrees Fahrenheit, and one theory was that most of the animal life had gone deep; another was that the drought experienced that summer had lowered water levels to the extent that salmon were hampered in their spawning runs and were not in the usual shallow areas of the lake to bring Nessie from the depths in order to feed. The 108,000 photographs taken by the strobe cameras had turned up scarcely any trout, salmon, or eels, let alone a monster. A high-resolution infrared instrument, designed to detect temperature differences of less than one degree, created by the creature's exhalations, had also failed. The most substantial sonar discovery was a sunken Wellington bomber that had been ditched over the lake during a training mission in 1940.

Yet the expedition could not be considered a disappointment, for there had been a number of fascinating and tantalizing occurrences. Around midnight on June 16, for example, Charles Wyckoff was watching the television screen when he noticed that the nearby time-lapse camera was fading out, as if silt were clouding the picture. That was odd because there was nothing nearby to roil the water—at least that he knew of. He triggered the strobe, but the water was now so murky that he could barely make out the powerful light. A few minutes later the water had cleared sufficiently that he could again see the time-lapse camera—and it seemed to be moving violently off-screen to the right. He hit the strobe button again. The camera was gone.

An hour later, around 1:00, the camera came back in-

In a project known as Operation Deepscan, twenty-four sonar-equipped boats swept much of the twenty-four-mile length of Loch Ness in October 1987, creating a sonar curtain (below) that no moving object could escape. While no definite evidence of Nessie was uncovered, some researchers claim engine noise would have driven such a creature into hiding.

to view, apparently none the worse for wear. Wrote Dennis Meredith, managing editor of the magazine *Technology Review* and the expedition's chronicler: "The episode was over, leaving Charlie mystified. He had no idea whether he had encountered the creature. He was exhausted and went to bed. It had been a harrowing night."

There were other strange doings as well. In late June, the scientists set up one of their sonar devices to scan the area around the suspended cameras. Anything swimming by would show up as a trace. On June 20, they noticed two traces curving across the screen—perhaps a pair of large salmon. Then on June 24, they began picking up different traces—large solid objects much bigger than fish. The objects presented about a six-foot-wide target to the sonar beam and appeared at 7:18, 8:52, and 8:56 a.m., remaining in the beam for only a few seconds before disappearing. On June 25 and 28, other large targets appeared in the sonar beam, too far away to be photographed.

Then at 10:44 p.m. on June 30, Charles Wyckoff's wife, Helen, was monitoring the sonar and observed a large object enter the beam at about 120 yards out and gradually move closer until it stopped and hovered 80 yards away from the camera. It was still too far away to photograph, and after a short time, it moved back and away. Finally, at 5:00 a.m. on July 1, the strongest trace of all—a target thirty feet wide—cut across the sonar beam about 100 yards from the camera. Charles Wyckoff was on duty and watched with rising excitement as the thing remained in the beam for about three minutes. Then he bolted from the cottage and rushed to the pier—"to be greeted," wrote Meredith, "only by the gray mists hovering over the still waters."

The last traces were observed on July 4, and after that

there was nothing. Had the monster arrived at last, only to be put off by all the activity around the site? No one could know. But when the members left, wrote Meredith, "They took with them the dead certainty that there *was* a Loch Ness monster. Any doubts had evaporated under the careful examinations of the past evidence, the talks with the reliable local citizens, and their own evidence. Except for the sonar traces, the 1976 evidence for the animal was undoubtedly inadmissible scientifically. But in any scientific controversy, the admissible evidence is merely the tip of the intellectual iceberg. Beneath the solid, tangible proof, there is always the huge mass of hints and indications, and even hunches, that support a theory."

For those impeccable scientists, Edgerton and Wyckoff, the case was convincing enough for them to write the words *Nessiteras rhombopteryx*—the Ness marvel with the diamond-shaped fin—beside the sonar traces; that was the scientific name Sir Peter Scott had given the beast when he himself became sure of its existence in 1962.

And the evidence was enough for Rines, who has continued every summer to press his quest for the monster against the most discouraging odds. In 1979, he announced plans to enlist the aid of a pair of dolphins, equipped with sonar-triggered cameras and strobe lights. The idea was that the dolphins, with their superb natural senses, would find the monster, at which point the strobes would illuminate and the cameras document its existence. But before the dolphins could be transported to Loch Ness, one of them died and Rines decided to cancel the attempt.

Meanwhile, the British had come back. Low in funds and morale, the LNI had shut down its camp and disbanded. But two years later many of the same people regrouped and moved on to Loch Morar, on the west coast of Scotland, where the monster Morag was said to dwell. According to legend, a sighting of Morag was an omen of death for a member of the Gilles clan. But for investigators, it breathed new life into the search for lake monsters.

They had been following the developments at Loch Morar since 1969, when word reached them that Morag had made a violent appearance. On a summer evening, according to the report, Morag rammed into a boat occupied by two truck drivers who were returning from a fishing trip. One of them, Duncan McDonnell, tried to beat it off with an oar, but the oar snapped. It was only after his friend, William Simpson, grabbed his rifle and fired a shot that the beast submerged.

For several summers, the Loch Ness hunters had periodically interrupted their quest to take a busman's holiday to Loch Morar to join the search for Morag. In 1974, they shifted their headquarters there and renamed their endeavor the Loch Ness and Morar Project, directed by Adrian Shine. But while the researchers' loyalties were now divided, they resumed work at Loch Ness, and in 1982, the lake was again under scrutiny from water and air.

That summer, the Loch Ness and Morar Project undertook a 1,500-hour, day-and-night sonar sweep of Morar's waters. The number of tracings was exceptionally high, and most of them could not be attributed to fish—or, at least, not to any known species of fish. But nothing appeared on the surface or in front of the underwater cameras—possibly because a Goodyear blimp arrived from its base in Italy to join in the hunt and spent fifteen hours hovering over the lake. Its gargantuan shadow could have been enough to frighten any creature back to its lair.

The lake was relatively quiet for five more years. Then in the summer of 1987, it became the center of attention again. The International Society of Cryptozoology, an organization of zoologists and others interested in the science of hidden animals, held its annual meeting at the Royal Museum of Scotland in Edinburgh and devoted a full day to discussions of the search for Nessie.

Later that year, another massive expedition was launched under Shine's supervision. Called Operation Deepscan, it was the most comprehensive sonar probe ever undertaken of the vast lake. Two dozen boats, lined up port to starboard, dropped a sweeping sonar curtain into the lake. For three days, the flotilla moved up and down Loch Ness like a waterborne chorus line, continuously scanning the depths. Only three sonar contacts were registered, but one of them was baffling even to the somewhat skeptical engineers who had supplied the sonar. Not far from Urquhart Castle, the sonar's graph recorder showed something large moving slowly more than 600 feet below the surface. Said Darrell Lowrance, president of a Tulsa, Oklahoma, electronics company—who provided funding and sonar equipment for the project: "There's something here that we don't understand, and there's something here that's larger than a fish, maybe some species that hasn't been detected before. I don't know."

Equally intriguing, Shine's expedition also produced an image, variously identified as a rotting tree stump or a rock outcropping, that seemed to resemble the celebrated 1975 Gargoyle Photograph by Robert Rines. There was nothing to prove that the monster existed, and nothing to prove that it did not. Inevitably, for the monster hunters, that meant adjourning the search for another summer, when modern technology might finally prevail. Or perhaps the monster itself would relent and pose briefly for one perfect photographic session that would establish its presence beyond all doubt.

To be sure, the naysayers were in the majority, and their numbers were growing as the might of science was increasingly brought to bear on the mystery, without much result. Nevertheless, it remained difficult to discredit all the evidence—all the sightings, the snapshots, the intriguing sonar returns—that had accumulated over the last half century. Nor, for that matter, was it easy to dismiss out of hand the folk wisdom of Highlanders such as the old patriarch who some years ago remarked, "There's many a queer thing in that loch."

An Elusive Creature of the Congo

For more than two hundred years, tales of a claw-footed, hippopotamus-size creature with a long neck and tail have spread across central Africa. Canoes coming near the beasts are instantly attacked, the stories say, and all aboard are killed. It is also reported that a pygmy tribe speared one of the animals to death and later feasted on its carcass; their village was soon plagued with unusual house fires, illnesses, and deaths. This fearsome tropical monster is known to the Congolese people as Mokele-mbembe.

In 1980 and 1981, American biochemist Roy P. Mackal mounted two expeditions into the treacherous Likouala swamp region, a vast area of the People's Republic of the Congo that few humans have penetrated, hoping to find and photograph one of the elusive creatures. Working with his colleagues James Powell and Richard Greenwell, Mackal collected dozens of firsthand descriptions of the Mokele-mbembe from widely dispersed Congo natives. Many of the reports were strikingly similar. And the animal's size, eating habits, and general appearance proved remarkably consistent with those of a small sauropod dinosaur, a creature thought to have been extinct for more than 60 million years.

Mackal himself did not see the supposedly living dinosaur, but Congolese biologist Marcellin Agnagna, who accompanied the American on his second expedition, claims to have spotted one on a subsequent trip. The tantalizing hunt for solid evidence of Mokele-mbembe is chronicled on the following six pages.

Roy Mackal (second from left) travels the Ubangi River with Richard Greenwell and Marcellin Agnagna (second and third from right).

Thick jungles and steamy rivers and swamps cover much of the African Congo, reputedly the lair of the creature called Mokele-mbembe. Deadly snakes and crocodiles, swarms of mosquitoes, and oppressive heat and humidity add to the inhospitality of the region. These formidable conditions, posing considerable hazard to explorers, have remained virtually unchanged for millions of years, suggesting to some cryptozoologists that it would be possible for dinosaur-like animals to have survived in the Congo and lived on until the present day.

CONGO

Mackal examines an alleged Mokele-mbembe footprint. It could also, he noted, have been the print of a small elephant.

Lush vegetation overhangs a reputed Mokele-mbembe lair along the Likouala-aux-Herbes River. A Congolese army officer claims to have come within thirty feet of one of the creatures near this spot. He told Mackal that the animals dig cavelike hideaways in the riverbanks.

The landolphia fruit (right), said to be the herbivorous Mokele-mbembe's primary food, has an "acrid sweet taste," according to Mackal, "unlike anything else I had ever eaten." When waterways became too shallow and clogged for the dugout, the Mackal party sometimes had to slog through the swamps in waist-deep water. Unnerving encounters with such snakes as poisonous gaboons and mambas made progress all the more difficult. Below, accompanied by a guide, Richard Greenwell tries to keep his camera dry during an excursion to look for lowland gorillas—animals that proved every bit as elusive as Mokele-mbembe.

Marcellin Agnagna shows a sketch of the creature he claims to have spotted in a Congolese lake in 1983. Camera problems prevented the biologist from bringing back hard evidence, but he had no doubt that "the animal we saw was Mokele-mbembe."

An artist's rendering of Mokele-mbembe commissioned by Roy Mackal shows a creature resembling a sauropod dinosaur. Of the likelihood that such an animal still walks the earth, Mackal has said, "I admit that my own views are tinged with some romanticism, but certainly not to the extent that I would endure extreme hardship, even risk my life, to pursue a dream with no basis in reality."

CHAPTER 3

In Pursuit of Bigfoot and Yeti

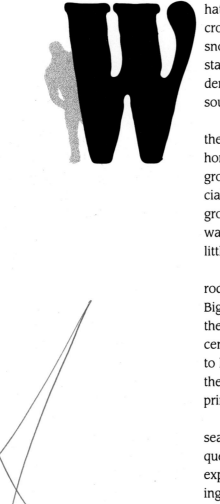

Whatever its nature, the creature was almost certainly female. She was crouched over a fallen tree alongside the river when she heard a horse snort. Startled, she rose up to her considerable full height and turned to stare across the sun-dappled water at the two mounted men who had blundered into her presence. The rushing of the stream must have muffled the sounds of their approach.

Her sudden, looming appearance—and possibly her smell—spooked the horses and set them to screaming and backing in fright. The nearest horse reared so high that its seasoned rider slipped from the saddle to the ground. The creature had seen enough. Appearing concerned but not especially alarmed, she began to lope away across the pebbles and the sandy ground. The dismounted horseman struggled to his feet and stumbled toward her, pointing something shiny in her direction, while his companion, a little farther off, fought to control his mount and a packhorse.

The man whose horse had thrown him was Roger Patterson, a former rodeo rider, a part-time inventor, and an avowed believer in the existence of Bigfoot—the generic popular name for a race of hairy primates said to live in the forests of the Pacific Northwest region of the United States and in adjacent Canada, where the creature is known as Sasquatch. Few people claim to have sighted the animals, and the chief evidence of their existence—and the source of their American name—is a series of improbably huge footprints found over the years in isolated, heavily forested areas.

Patterson—short, sinewy, and durable looking—had already been searching for Bigfoot for years, and now, in October of 1967, he was on his quest once again. With his friend Bob Gimlin, a construction worker and expert horseman, he had been camping out for more than seven days, looking for tracks in reputed Bigfoot territory—the wooded highlands of northern California near the Oregon border.

On Friday, October 20, at about 1:15 in the afternoon, with Gimlin leading the packhorse, the two riders had been picking their way northward along Bluff Creek, which flows eventually into the Klamath River. The shallow creek bed was about 100 feet wide; the creek itself was narrow and less than a foot deep, to their left. Ahead of them, a fifteen-foot-high tangle of logs and trees lay athwart the watercourse, obscuring their view.

Just as they had come abreast of the logs, they reported later, they had confronted, with terrifying suddenness, Patterson's long-sought quarry. The shiny object that Patterson dug out of his saddlebag when he regained his feet was a rented 16-mm motion picture camera. In the hopes of producing a documentary film for television, Patterson had been taking scenic shots of Bigfoot country and keeping the camera at hand for just such a circumstance.

Patterson had started the camera running and had charged with it through the wet sand toward the creature—he had no doubt that it was a Bigfoot. As he plunged along, waving the camera erratically, the creature moved away behind some low piles of logs and scrub.

"Cover me!" shouted Patterson. Gimlin drew his rifle from its scabbard, holding the weapon only at the ready—the men had agreed earlier never to shoot a Bigfoot unless it threatened them. Patterson stopped running, crouched, and kept the camera pointed as best he could at the retreating figure which, at one point, swiveled her torso and head and looked back at her pursuers as she continued to stride away from them.

"Oh, my God, I'm out of film!" Patterson cried. He had used most of it shooting scenery, and the rest of their film supply was in the saddlebags on Patterson's horse, which had now bolted away out of sight, along with the pack animal. After some moments of confusion, the men decided it would be wiser to collect their horses than to pursue the creature into the trees.

By the time they retrieved the animals from a meadow about a mile downstream and returned to the site, the creature was long gone. But Patterson had what he had come for; in the sandy creek bed was a clear set of Bigfoot prints. He and Gimlin quickly made plaster casts of the inch-deep impressions. They were fourteen and a half inches long and five inches wide, and the creature's stride measured forty to forty-two inches.

But the real bonanza the men brought back from their expedition was the film—jumpy and hard to follow at the start, it was a mere twenty-four feet in length, running for just a minute or so of viewing time. But it was unprecedented in the often-bizarre search for evidence of Bigfoot. It showed a burly, broad-shouldered creature with large, pendulous breasts. Dark, reddish black hair covered her entire body, except for parts of the face, her nipples, the palms of her hands, and the soles of her feet. Her head was carried so low on her shoulders that she appeared neckless, and her forehead sloped back from her eyebrows to a high point at the back of her head, reminiscent of the crested, massive skull of a gorilla.

The creature loped away from the camera, swinging thick arms that were proportionately longer than a human's, pumping what seemed to be immensely powerful legs. Both men recalled being struck by the smoothness of her gait as she calmly but quickly moved away from them. Later analysis of the film indicated that as each leg alternately received her weight, the knee remained bent, somewhat like that of a cross-country skier. In contrast, humans normally take the body's weight on straight legs, bobbing up and down with each stride.

Although glimpsed only for a moment in the flesh, the creature was eventually viewed by millions of people as her image flickered across their television screens. Those twenty-four feet of controversial film excited and intrigued the general public. Most experts dismissed the whole episode as a carefully contrived hoax. But some, after careful analysis, accepted the film as evidence that a race of giant, humanlike monsters—serene, secretive, and immensely strong—might be found roaming the remaining patches of the planet's wilderness.

Throughout history, similar beings have been reported in the remote corners of most of the earth's continents. Tales suggest that they have always been there, these hairy, bipedal creatures, occupying a niche somewhere between humans and the rest of the animal kingdom, lurking in the farthest outskirts of civilization. Ancient Babylon had its

Enkidu, the hairy denizen of the epic of Gilgamesh, and the Anglo-Saxons thrilled to the menace of the giant Grendel, slain by Beowulf. Satyrs and other woods-dwelling beings haunted the Greeks. A dictionary compiled during China's Chou dynasty in 200 BC described the *feifei*, a hairy, ten-foot-tall creature that resembled humans as well as orangutans but had a taste for human flesh.

Legends are no longer transmitted from generation to generation over lonely campfires. Civilization, with its advanced methods of communication, has pushed its way into virtually every corner of a crowded globe, but these creatures will not go away. In an age of satellite surveillance and mechanized travel, strange beasts like Bigfoot are still spotted beyond the megalopolis and the freeway. In remote areas of central Asia, there are persistent reports of a race of subhumans called Almas, living in sociable groups and, in at least one case, mating with humans. Southern Malaysia is said to be the home of Orang-Dalam, a hairy, ten-foot creature that exudes a nauseating smell.

Most scientists greet such reports with derision. They will grant that there are many new species of insects, rodents, reptiles, and perhaps even birds to be discovered deep in the tropical rain forests, but they insist that the large animals of the world have all been found and cataloged. To be sure, a few sizable mammals turned up for the first time as late as the twentieth century *(page 20)*, but according to the vast majority of zoologists, the world has been too much traveled, too well explored, for something as big as a Sasquatch to suddenly appear in some wilderness area. Indeed, there is no true wilderness remaining, some scientists maintain, now that satellites are capable of beaming back detailed photographs of nearly every square yard of the planet's varied surface.

And yet, reports of startling encounters with hairy beasts keep coming. Some of the accounts are shown to be fraudulent, some mistaken, and yet others remain to tantalize the imagination, to challenge the conviction that the world holds no more surprises. Even a few respected scientists believe that something unexpected, something

strangely like a human, dwells in the wild places. Only a few decades ago, they point out, a hermit living in a shack went utterly undetected for more than ten years—in a small park in the city of Portland, Oregon. Surely, a cunning creature of the wild could live in secret far from the regular haunts of humans.

Perhaps the most widely celebrated of the elusive wilderness monsters is the so-called Abominable Snowman—or as Nepal's mountain-dwelling Sherpas say, *yeh-teh*, or Yeti—whose tracks have been often discovered in the frigid lands of perpetual snow in the Himalayan regions of India, Nepal, and Tibet. According to locals, the Yeti is but one of several unidentified creatures that inhabit the highlands of southern Asia.

One of the first westerners to take note of the Yeti may have been a British army major named L. A. Waddell. In 1889, Waddell found what he took to be large footprints in the snow on a high peak northeast of Sikkim. Ten years later, in a memoir, he wrote: "These were alleged to be the trail of the hairy wild man believed to live amongst the eternal snows. The belief in these creatures is universal among Tibetans." But this account—as well as a smattering of other reports—was ignored in Europe and America for decades, until the creature was popularized by an unwitting error in the translation of its Nepalese name.

In 1921, members of a British expedition climbing the north face of Mount Everest noted, as they reached 17,000 feet, some dark figures moving around on a snowfield above them. When the explorers reached the spot, the creatures were not there but apparently had left behind some huge, humanlike footprints in the snow. The leader of the expedition, Lt. Col. Charles Kenneth Howard-Bury of the British army, later spoke of the incident with journalists in India, noting that his Sherpa guides called the elusive creatures *metoh-kangmi*. In fact, the name was a generic Nepalese term for several mountain creatures said to roam the area, but in the course of transmission to the world the

A Jungle Mystery

When Swiss geologist François de Loys and his expedition emerged from the jungles of Colombia and Venezuela in 1920, they told of having killed one of a couple of enraged apelike creatures that had attacked them.

The men placed the creature atop a fuel crate and photographed it, propping a stick under its chin to hold it upright. The strange animal was reportedly just over five feet tall —a foot and a half taller than the largest American monkeys—and had a strangely human expression. Skeptics at once disputed de Loys's estimate of the animal's height. One expert, however, figured the creature's size based on the dimensions of a standard fuel crate and agreed with the geologist's account. A decade of study yielded no insight into the beast's identity. But in 1931, an Italian anthropological team ventured into the jungle of British Guiana, and while the scientists did not observe a creature matching de Loys's description, they did turn up eyewitness accounts startlingly similar to de Loys's.

word was mistakenly thought to be Tibetan and was translated as "Abominable Snowman."

Reporters were entranced, newspaper editors were delighted, and the public was fascinated. Before long the creature, thanks to its catchy name, became an international sensation. And mountaineers, always interested enough in the conquest of Everest and other great Himalayan peaks, would now have another reason to explore the high snowfields—to find the Abominable Snowman.

But many who were prepared to grant the possibility of the creatures' existence thought they were misnamed. While such large animals might feasibly have reason to venture into the snowfields—to store their food, to find a particular kind of delicacy such as vitamin-rich lichen on rocks, or simply to travel through a high pass—it did not stand to reason that they could find enough food to live there permanently. They would have to be denizens of the high valley forests, not "snowmen."

Whatever their abode, reported sightings of large tracks, and of the great creatures themselves, began to accumulate. In 1925, an adventuresome Greek photographer named N. A. Tombazi was 15,000 feet up in the mountains of Sikkim when his porters began shouting and pointing. About 200 to 300 yards away, he glimpsed a figure that he later described as "exactly like a human being, walking upright and stopping occasionally to uproot or pull at some dwarf rhododendron bushes."

The unclothed creature quickly disappeared, but Tombazi later found its tracks in the snow. Although shaped like a human footprint, these impressions were both shorter— only about six inches in length—and broader, measuring four inches at the widest part of the foot.

This and other reports that followed in the 1930s gave rise to the thought that there might be more than one kind of creature ranging through the snowy mountains. The tracks reported by Tombazi were smaller than those of a human; others, such as those seen by Howard-Bury, were larger. But all of the tracks resembled human footprints in that they showed five toes and were plantigrade—that is,

the entire sole of the foot touched the ground with each step the creature took.

Indeed, the Sherpas had always spoken of at least two types of creature, and used different names in referring to each. All of them were known as *teh*, the Sherpa word for a flesh-and-blood animal. But one kind, a large beast that travels on all fours and stands up only when it runs, they called *dzu-teh*. Some researchers think this is the relatively common Himalayan black bear that often preys on the yak herds of the region.

For the other, smaller denizen of the high places, the Sherpas have two terms. One, *meh-teh*, means man-beast. The other, more familiar term *yeh-teh* refers to an animal that inhabits rocky places. The Sherpas think of this smaller animal as a nearly human-size, erect creature that lives at the tree line, often venturing upward into the perpetual snow, sometimes moving down the mountainside to pilfer food from a village or prey on a yak herd. Described as having pointed heads, long arms hanging below the knees, and a covering of reddish hair, the Yeti would seem to be a smaller version of North America's Bigfoot, though most investigators insist that the two creatures are entirely different.

To the Sherpas, the Yeti is a familiar figure that they have incorporated into their folklore with more humor than dread. The breasts of the female Yeti, it is said, are so pendulous that in order to run the creature must sling them over her shoulder. Sherpa children are often frightened into obedience by references to these monsters, but they are also advised how to escape their clutches—run downhill, they

A Tibetan lama displays a centuries-old sacred scalp, supposedly that of a Yeti, in 1960. Scientists later determined that the scalp belonged to a serow, a member of the goat-antelope family.

are told, because in downhill pursuit a Yeti's hair tends to fall over its face.

During the international strife and global war in the late 1930s and 1940s, the abode of the Yeti was largely forgotten by the outside world. But when peace returned, attention was once again directed toward that high and desolate part of the planet. One reason was the drive of adventurers to scale unconquered peaks. The great barrier of mountains that extends from the Karakoram range of Pakistan to the Himalayas attracted a number of mountain climbers. The ultimate challenge for them was Mount Everest, at 29,028 feet the world's highest mountain, lying athwart the Nepal-Tibet border in the heart of Yeti country.

In 1951, the Everest Reconnaissance Expedition set out to evaluate routes for an attempt to ascend Everest. At 18,000 feet, two of the climbers encountered fresh tracks, which they followed along the edge of the Menlung Glacier for nearly a mile. According to expedition leader Eric Shipton, writing later in the *Times of London,* "the tracks were mostly distorted by melting into oval impressions, slightly longer and a good deal broader than those made by our large mountain boots. But here and there where the snow covering the ice was thin, we came upon a well-preserved impression of the creature's foot. It showed three broad 'toes' and a broad 'thumb' to the side." The clearest of the impressions measured thirteen by eight inches.

Shipton was a seasoned climber who had scaled mountains throughout the world, and his experiences could not be taken lightly. The publication of his report, accompanied by photographs of the tracks, caused a new explosion of interest in the Yeti. Several expeditions were mounted, including one ambitious effort financed in 1954 by the London *Daily Mail*. Led by reporter Ralph Izzard, the team made an effort to achieve scientific plausibility by including two zoologists. But the results of the search were disappointing—perhaps because it was conducted for the most part in the snowfields instead of in the high forests and rocky places where, presumably, Yetis spend most of their time. The explorers found some ambiguous footprints and a few reputed Yeti scalps that, embarrassingly, turned out to be pieces of goatskin.

During the following months, several additional sightings of Yeti tracks were reported, all the way from the western Karakoram to the easternmost Himalayas. But skeptics pointed out that melting snow can enlarge small, well-defined tracks, transforming them into bigger, less well-defined ones. They also called attention to the fact that bears of the region, when walking, place the hind foot in the spot just relinquished by the forefoot, often leaving an impression that resembles a large human print. The evidence was thus inconclusive.

In 1957, an American millionaire, Tom Slick, who had made his fortune from aviation, oil, and other endeavors, financed the first of three major expeditions to the Himalayas to find a Yeti. None of his three efforts found much more by way of evidence than had the *Daily Mail* expedition. But neither did they dispel the persistent belief that there was something to the Yeti that went beyond local legend and imagination.

That belief was dealt a considerable blow when Sir Edmund Hillary, knighted for his conquest of Everest in 1953, returned from the Himalayan Scientific and Mountaineering Expedition of 1960-1961. In addition to conducting research on human physiology at high altitudes, Hillary and his team investigated the question of the Yeti. They found a few of the footprints—but the renowned Hil-

Sir Edmund Hillary displays an artist's conception of a Yeti, the beast he hoped to find on a 1960 Himalayan expedition. During the trek Hillary examined footprints, furs, and scalps, but concluded there was no scientific basis for the Yeti legend.

lary pronounced them to be ordinary animal tracks enlarged and distorted by melting. The expedition also borrowed a supposed Yeti scalp from a Buddhist monastery, but the scalp turned out to be made of the skin of a serow, an ungainly goatlike animal of the region.

Hillary noted that Sherpas make little distinction between their metaphysical world and objective reality. They firmly believe, for example, that the Yeti can make itself invisible and then reappear at will. In Hillary's view, it all amounted to nothing more than a "fascinating fairy tale, born of the rare and frightening view of strange animals, molded by superstition, and enthusiastically nurtured by Western expeditions."

That same year, a respected British primatologist, William C. Osman Hill, sprang to the Yeti's defense and labeled Hillary's conclusions "rather hasty." Hill found the evidence of the Yeti's existence convincing, but he said the animal was clearly a creature of the "rhododendron thickets of the lower parts of the valleys, and it is here that future search should be directed." But, perhaps as a consequence of Hillary's well-publicized skepticism, organized searches for the elusive creature became rare. Although occasional reports of tracks found and sightings made continued to trickle in throughout the 1960s and 1970s and into the 1980s, they remain inconclusive.

Equally inconclusive are recurrent reports from the expansive land to the north of the Yeti's lofty country in central Asia, once the domain of Mongol warlords Genghis Khan and Tamerlane, today the heartland of the Soviet Union. This region of rugged mountain chains and broad deserts stretches from the Caucasus to the borders of China. It is

Soviet investigator Igor Bourstev ponders a skull said to be that of the son of a human male and an Almas female known as Zana. Reportedly held captive in the Caucasus during the nineteenth century, Zana supposedly bore four human-Almas babies.

widely believed to be the home of yet another race of wild, man-size creatures with dark pelts.

There are as many names for them as there are languages in this polyglot region: In Mongolia they are called the Almas, or wild men. Unlike the Yeti, little mythology or superstition surrounds the creatures; instead, they are taken for granted as a part of the local fauna. They are not considered to be anything to get excited about, merely a race of lesser humans who mean no harm. Indeed, for a long time they were listed in standard natural histories of the area, along with bears, deer, and other unexceptional creatures. And a staid nineteenth-century Mongolian book of natural pharmacology even reported that the gall of the Almas "cures jaundice."

One of the earliest descriptions of the Almas by a European was that of a Bavarian nobleman, Hans Schiltberger, who in the early fifteenth century was captured by Turks and given by them to a Mongol prince named Egidi. During his captivity, Schiltberger was taken to an area that is thought to be the Tien Shan range in western Mongolia.

"In the mountains themselves live wild people, who have nothing in common with other humans," Schiltberger wrote in 1430, some time after his escape from captivity. "A pelt covers the entire body of these creatures. Only the hands and face are free of hair. They run around in the hills like animals and eat foliage and grass and whatever else they can find. The lord of the territory made Egidi a present of a couple of forest people, a man and a woman. They had been caught in the wilderness, together with three untamed horses the size of asses."

Such a tale might well be dismissed as typical of the fabulous stories related by travelers of the time, but the mention of the small horses gave the report belated substantiation of a sort. In 1871, more than four centuries after Schiltberger's enforced sojourn in Mongolia, a Russian explorer named Nikolai Przewalski collected reports of "wild men" while on an expedition to Mongolia. In addition, he collected specimens of the wild, dun-colored Mongolian horse, presumably the "untamed horses" of Schiltberger's account, which is now known as Przewalski's horse.

Another report has it that in 1906, a Mongolian scholar named Badzar Baradiin was on a caravan through the desert of Alashan when, just before sunset, the caravan leader called out in fear. Everyone could see a hairy man standing on a hill, silhouetted against the sunset. The creature watched the expedition for a moment or two and then ran off into the desert. Afterward, when he was writing the official account of his expedition, Baradiin was reportedly instructed by the president of the Imperial Geographical Society to omit any mention of his encounter with an Almas. In recent years, however, some doubt has been cast on this sighting: Modern-day researchers who obtained Baradiin's original travel journal discovered that it contains no reference to such an event.

Whatever the truth about Baradiin's experience, a handful of Russian and Mongolian scholars have continued to take an interest in the Almas question, usually without governmental encouragement. The descriptions they have collected are remarkably similar. In general, Almas are said to be of medium human height—about five feet, five inches—and are covered with dark, often reddish hair. Their long arms reach below their knees, and they have stooped shoulders and narrow chests; they walk with their knees flexed, and are reported to run awkwardly at best—although they generally seem to run fast enough to have avoided capture. The forehead reportedly slopes backward from a bony crest over the eyes, and the lower jaw is massive but chinless. The feet are broad, with splayed toes; the big toe is smaller than a human's and is sometimes set apart from the other toes. The hands are humanlike, however, with long fingers.

According to the reports, Almas are generally nocturnal and stay away from humans, although every now and then they are sighted in the vicinity of farms and have been said to raid cornfields. Usually, the creatures are seen one at a time or in pairs, and at a distance. A typical sighting was reported in 1963 by Ivan Ivlov, a Russian pediatrician

This footprint, shown actual size, is said to have been left by an Almas, the legendary wild man of central Asia. Soviet researchers stud

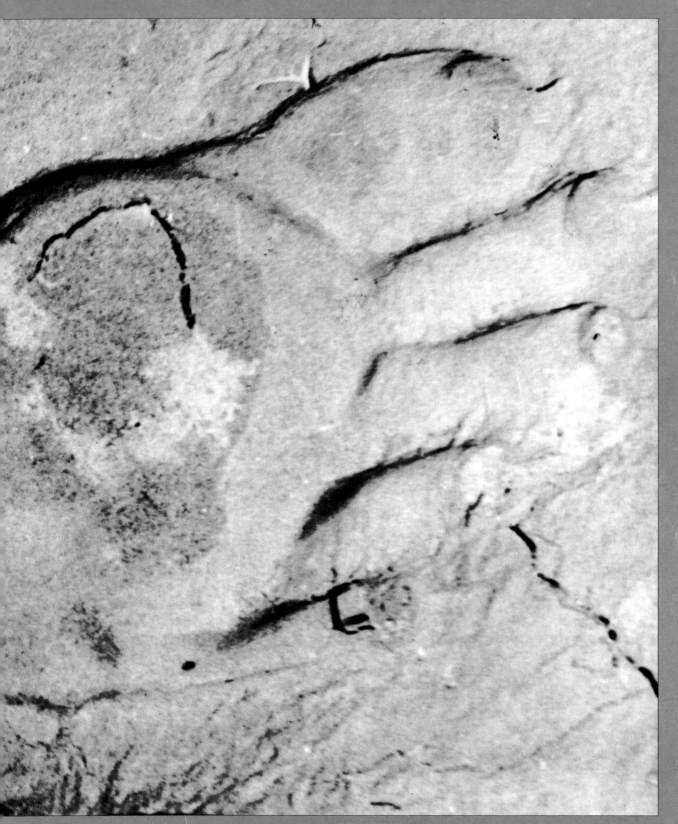

witness reports and sketched the Almas (inset) as a robust creature with sloping forehead, bulging brows, and massive lower jaw.

working in Mongolia. Ivlov had heard about the Almas but was highly skeptical. Then one day, while traveling in the Altai mountains of southern Mongolia, he claimed to have spotted an Almas family—a male, female, and child—about half a mile distant. According to Ivlov's account, he was able to watch them through his binoculars for some time, until they moved away behind a rock.

Occasionally, there are reports that one of the Almas has been captured. In about 1910, for example, a Russian zoologist named V. A. Khaklov met a Kazakh herdsman who claimed that he had once observed a female Almas over a period of several weeks. She had been captured by some farmers and chained to a mill, he said, and was later set free. Her physical description contained nothing new, but the herdsman offered rare details of Almas behavior.

As Khaklov recorded the herdsman's account: "This creature was usually quite silent, but she screeched and bared her teeth on being approached. She had a peculiar way of lying down, or sleeping; she squatted on her knees and elbows, resting her forehead on the ground, and her hands were folded over the back of her head. She would eat only raw meat, some vegetables and grain, and sometimes insects which she caught. When drinking water she would lap in animal fashion, or sometimes dip her arm into the water and lick her fur."

The most intriguing account of an Almas, however, is the story of Zana, a female that is said to have lived out her adult life in the late nineteenth century as a slave on a farm in the Caucasus. No one knows where she was captured or how many times she changed hands. But eventually, as an adult, she was reportedly taken in chains by a man named Edgi Genaba and put in a stone pen on his farm on the River Mokvi. For a time, Zana seemed so vicious and violent that no one on the farm would dare enter the enclosure; her food was simply thrown over the wall. She slept in a hole that she had dug in the dirt. After three years of this type of close and solitary confinement, she had become docile enough to be tethered in a fenced enclosure and soon was allowed to move about freely.

Her skin was dark brown and she was covered with reddish black hair; a shock of black hair on her head hung down like a mane. Her face was described as terrifying; her large teeth were set in a powerful jaw, and she had high cheekbones, a flat nose, and red-tinged eyes. She was large and extremely strong.

Although Zana never learned to talk, she made muttering sounds. Eventually, she did learn to do various chores at her master's command, but only outdoors—she could not endure heated rooms. And she had a peculiar habit that would in time give Almas researchers a clue to her possible origins; she spent a great deal of time determinedly grinding round stones against each other and banging them together.

In 1964, a Russian historian named Boris Porshnev visited the place where Zana had reportedly lived, hoping to gather firsthand accounts of her from the townspeople. The men and women of the Caucasus are noted for their longevity, and Porshnev talked to several centenarians who claimed to have known her and attended her funeral. Most intriguing of all, perhaps, he even visited two of Zana's supposed grandchildren.

Zana, it was said, had become pregnant several times, evidently by different men. She would give birth unassisted, and at first would carry the infant to the river to wash it. But the newborn half-breeds did not survive immersion in the cold water, and the villagers began to take her babies away to be reared by human families. In all, two sons and two daughters are said to have survived.

According to the villagers, Zana's offspring differed only slightly from other children. Their appearance was not only human, but almost ordinary—except for their swarthiness. They learned to speak normally, and their behavior was acceptable, if somewhat unruly. The younger son, named Khvit, had been a farm worker, and was recalled as "extremely strong, difficult to deal with, and wild and turbulent." He had a high-pitched voice and was noted as an accomplished singer.

The Enigmatic Iceman

In late 1968, the Scottish-born writer and zoologist Ivan T. Sanderson and his French colleague Bernard Heuvelmans learned that a strange apelike creature, frozen in a block of ice, had been exhibited at a Chicago livestock fair. Details of the creature's appearance intrigued the two scientists, and they contacted the manager of the exhibit, Frank Hansen. He encouraged the scientists to examine the so-called Iceman at his farm near Winona, Minnesota.

According to Hansen, a veteran carnival huckster who at times varied his tale, the creature had been found off the coast of Siberia by either Russian sealers or Japanese whalers, floating in a 6,000-pound block of ice. Later, the Iceman had turned up in a Hong Kong emporium, where the creature was purchased by an agent for an anonymous American millionaire. Hansen subsequently rented the Iceman and exhibited him at carnivals for thirty-five cents a peek.

Sanderson and Heuvelmans spent two days studying and photographing the specimen through the glass lid of its insulated, refrigerated coffin. The thick ice, frosted in some areas and nearly opaque in others, obscured much of the creature and prevented close inspection. Nevertheless, Heuvelmans declared the frozen mass to be an unknown hominid, a type of Neanderthal man, and published his conclusions in a Belgian scientific journal. Sanderson believed the creature to be an "ultra-primitive, anthropoid-like primate" but felt further study was in order. He contacted the Smithsonian Institution and suggested that the museum study the Iceman.

When museum officials requested permission to examine the specimen, however, Hansen announced that it

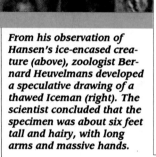

From his observation of Hansen's ice-encased creature (above), zoologist Bernard Heuvelmans developed a speculative drawing of a thawed Iceman (right). The scientist concluded that the specimen was about six feet tall and hairy, with long arms and massive hands.

had been returned to its owner and would probably not be exhibited again. He further explained that a synthetic copy of the original had been made, and this copy was now on exhibit.

With the genuine Iceman supposedly unavailable, the already-dubious Smithsonian experts prepared to bow out, but not before they expressed a few concerns to the Federal Bureau of Investigation. Evidently, Heuvelmans had noted in his examination of the creature what appeared to be a bullet hole through the right eye. If, as he and Sanderson concluded, the creature had been alive in recent times, the wound suggested foul play. The FBI

declined to be drawn into the case, but Hansen added the bureau's prestige to his ballyhoo. Displaying his model in a Minnesota shopping center, the showman proclaimed that the beast had been "investigated by the FBI."

Meanwhile, inquiries by Sanderson and the Smithsonian had uncovered three West Coast companies that claimed to have fashioned an Iceman for Hansen out of latex and hair as early as one year before the two zoologists heard of Hansen's exhibit. More intriguing, when Hansen took his show on the road again in 1969, it appeared that the creature was indeed different from the one inspected by Sanderson and Heuvelmans. For some, this confirmed Hansen's assertion that there was a copy and an original; others, however, suspected that a frozen, flesh-and-blood Iceman had never existed and that there had instead been several latex versions.

Increasing incredulity did not deter Hansen. He soon surfaced with yet another story about the Iceman's origins, meant to account for the apparent bullet wound. This time Hansen confessed to having shot a strange creature in the woods of northern Minnesota while on a hunting trip. He left the beast in the woods, he said, but retrieved it later that winter. Hansen took the corpse home and placed it in his freezer until, seven years later, he decided to exhibit the icy remains at carnivals and fairs.

In spite of Hansen's constantly revised tales, Sanderson and Heuvelmans stood firm, convinced that they had studied a strange, rare creature. But the truth about the Iceman's identity has remained uncertain, cloaked in mystery and perhaps still frozen in a block of murky ice.

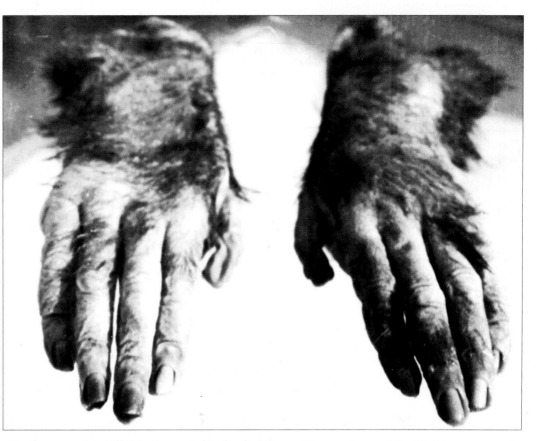

The discovery late in 1980 of the preserved hands (right) and feet of a supposed Chinese Wildman sparked new interest in the legendary creature. This particular beast—described as three feet tall, with long brown hair and a humanlike face—was killed in 1957. Analysis of the severed appendages showed they belonged to a large macaque monkey, possibly of a new subspecies.

Porshnev reported visiting two of Khvit's children a few years after the death of their father. "From the moment I saw Zana's grandchildren," Porshnev wrote, "I was impressed by their dark skin and negroid looks. Shalikula, the grandson, has unusually powerful jaw muscles, and he can pick up a chair, with a man sitting on it, with his teeth."

During the next few years, Porshnev and a colleague made repeated attempts to find Zana's remains in the Genaba family graveyard, by then overgrown with weeds. Although they did uncover the vaguely Neanderthaloid remains of what may have been one of Zana's children, they never found the supposed Almas herself.

Despite the lack of concrete evidence, the story of Zana convinced Porshnev that the Almas are relict Neanderthals, a belief shared by some other researchers. The original Neanderthals, who roamed what is now central Asia and Europe before being supplanted by Cro-Magnon man about 40,000 years ago, are considered by most paleoanthropologists to have been a human subspecies, not very different biologically from ourselves.

The presumed closeness of the relationship means that humans and Neanderthals could have interbred; indeed, some experts believe the ancient race was not extinguished but was merely absorbed by the dominant human line. Because it is generally not possible for an individual of one species to produce viable young by mating with an individual of another species, the existence of Zana's grandchildren is thought by some to lend credence to Porshnev's view that the Almas are remnant Neanderthals. And, of course, there was Zana's obsession with banging round rocks together—perhaps, according to Porshnev, as if to fashion stone tools, an urge that

might also link her with ancestors of the Pleistocene epoch.

More recently, a Russian anatomist and mountain climber named Marie-Jeanne Koffmann, has spent many years collecting and analyzing accounts of the Almas, using sophisticated statistical procedures. Her analyses have added new detail to the picture of the Almas. She has concluded that it is a territorial animal and that it migrates up and down, from high forest to valley floor, with the seasonal changes in vegetation.

Koffmann has also proposed that human population pressures in the Caucasus are squeezing the Almas population to the point of vanishing. Where sightings were once plentiful, they are now few: "We witness," she wrote in 1984, "the end of the Caucasus hominoid." Similar tales of woe are heard from its supposed Mongolian haunts, where the Almas might soon join Przewalski's horse on the roster of animals that are extinct in the wild.

Whatever their fate, the Almas remain an enigma shrouded by official Soviet skepticism and secrecy. If there is any convincing physical evidence—such as a body or a living captive—the rest of the world has not been told of it.

A breed of hairy hominoid is also said to roam the People's Republic of China, where the creature has been given the descriptive name of Wildman. Sightings of Wildmen have been reported for centuries, and are particularly plentiful in the southern tier of Chinese provinces, where enormous forests cloak the landscape.

The first recorded sighting by a scientist occurred in 1950, when a geologist named Fan Jingquan reported his distant observation of two Wildmen—a mother and son—in a forest in Shanxi Province. In 1961, when road builders working in a thickly forested area of Yunnan Province reported that they had killed a female Wildman, the Chinese Academy of Sciences dispatched a team to the spot. The investigators found no body but concluded that the animal—which was only about four feet tall—probably had been an ordinary gibbon.

As elsewhere, most Chinese scientists were skeptical. But reports persisted. In 1976, for example, a caravan of foresters driving through the Shennongjia mountains of Hu-

bei Province came across a large, hairy creature standing in the road, lit by their headlights. Several men went to investigate, approaching to within a yard or two of the beast. They later telegraphed a report to the Chinese Academy of Sciences, insisting that the creature was not a bear or any other animal they knew.

A protracted hunt ensued, involving nearly a hundred scientists and their assistants, aided by army units, all of whom combed an area of 500 square miles for a period of two years. The leader of this search was Zhou Guoxing, a paleoanthropologist at the Beijing Natural History Museum, who was undaunted when the search turned up only indirect evidence of the creature—consisting chiefly of oversize footprints, strands of hair, and feces.

The publicity triggered many new reports. One intrigu-

Chinese peasant Gong Yulan shows scientists the tree where, in June 1976, she observed a shaggy, humanlike beast scratching its back. Hair recovered from the bark was judged that of an unknown higher primate.

According to hundreds of eyewitness reports, the rugged terrain of the Pacific Northwest (opposite) is home to Sasquatch—or Bigfoot. Shown here are sketches by some who claim to have seen such creatures.

ing account was related by a commune team leader, Pang Gensheng, who said he encountered a hairy Wildman while out chopping wood. Anything but reclusive, this specimen boldly approached the apprehensive Pang, who backed away until he was against the base of a cliff and could go no farther. The beast kept coming until it was only five feet away—at which point, Pang said, he raised his ax.

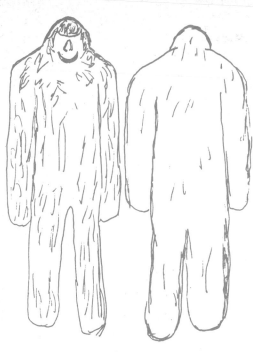

A Montana teenager drew two views of the Bigfoot he claimed to have seen in 1976.

The two stood thus for what Pang said was nearly an hour. Then he threw a rock, hitting the beast in the chest. It howled and scampered off muttering, pausing to lean briefly against a tree before it disappeared into a gully. Pang described his unexpected visitor as being seven feet tall with wide shoulders, a sloping forehead, and long arms.

William Roe allegedly saw this Sasquatch in British Columbia in 1955.

Dozens of similar reports, many sets of tracks, and other indirect evidence—such as hair that upon analysis seemed to be from no known animal—have convinced Zhou Guoxing and some other Chinese scientists that the Wildman exists. But Zhou freely admits that proving it is a frustrating task. Not only are there hoaxes and false leads to contend with, but as he puts it, the researchers themselves "are not always in a totally objective or scientific frame of mind."

Zhou demonstrated the necessary rigor in 1980, when he examined some preserved hands and feet that were supposed to be those of a Wildman. The scientist soon concluded that they were no such thing. Instead, Zhou concluded, they belonged to some type

This beast was reportedly spotted by an Oregon teacher in 1971.

of monkey, probably an unknown species of macaque—a creature whose existence could account for occasional reports of smaller-than-human Wildmen in the remote forests of southern China.

But Zhou still believes that the existence of a large, nocturnal, omnivorous primate in the thickets of the vast Chinese forests makes perfectly good biological and ecological sense. In most areas where Wildmen are reported today, the forest has changed little over the millennia. Clearly, this is a stable environment that could also be conducive to the persistence of animal life well adapted to it. And in a relatively recent geological epoch—the Pleistocene, which ended 10,000 years ago—one of the dominant animals in the region was evidently a large, apelike creature called *Gigantopithecus.*

Long presumed extinct, this giant is known to scientists only through fossilized jaws and teeth. Most of the species that shared the epoch with it have also disappeared. But, Zhou points out, not all. Among the known survivors are the tapir and the giant panda, an extremely elusive denizen of the high bamboo forests of Szechuan.

It seems reasonable to Zhou and others to think that *Gigantopithecus,* which some say was an ape and others argue was an early prehominid, continued to thrive in the remote forests of the region. Instead of dying out, these researchers surmise, the creature may have evolved into the Wildman of today, and—given the propensity of man and other animals to move widely across the surface of the earth—into the storied North American Sasquatch, or Bigfoot, as well.

No one knows exactly when humans first reached the North American continent. But there is little doubt that they came from

Oregon logger Jack Cochran spied this curious creature in 1974.

Asia and crossed the northern Pacific in the region of the Bering Strait, probably in pursuit of game. Their crossing was made possible, as was the migration of other species of mammals from time to time during thousands of years, when the advance of Ice Age glaciers resulted in a decrease in sea level so that a land bridge appeared between present-day Siberia and Alaska.

By about 10,000 years ago, people of Mongoloid stock had spread through North and South America. Perhaps they carried with them ancient tribal memories of giant hairy monsters whose unearthly howls had pierced the Asian night. Indeed, they may even have been preceded or followed by these very giants. At any rate, accounts of the giants have persisted among some American Indians; not in the desert areas or the plains, to be sure, but among those tribes that took up residence in forested lands, most notably the high forests of the Pacific Northwest.

From one of these tribes, the Salish of British Columbia, comes the popular name Sasquatch; the Huppas of northern California call it *oh-mah-ah,* shortened to *omah.* Here there is no linguistic confusion about snowmen; the various names mean, quite simply, "wild men of the woods." And it is in the continent's heavily wooded regions that later white immigrants have also encountered the creature or observed signs of its passage.

Apparently, reports of such encounters began in the nineteenth century. In 1811, while crossing the northern Rocky Mountains, a Canadian trader named David Thompson saw huge tracks, measuring some fourteen by eight inches, in the snow near what is now Jasper, Alberta. On July 4, 1884, a newspaper in Victoria, British Columbia, reported that a train crew had captured a short, long-armed, manlike creature covered with coarse black hair. They named the immensely powerful creature Jacko. Jacko's fate is not known; he simply disappeared from the record, either a chimpanzee escaped from a circus or, some suggest, a juvenile Sasquatch.

Over the decades, there were sporadic reports of similar encounters, most of them from British Columbia, many of them fantastic. One had to do with several hairy giants who attacked a prospector's shack near Kelso, Washington. But the world paid little heed to such stories; most people who thought about the Sasquatch at all relegated it to the realm of hoax, delusion, or Indian legend.

But in the early 1950s, when Eric Shipton's photograph of the huge Yeti track on Mount Everest drew international attention, a handful of North Americans began to look more closely at reports of their own legendary giant. One of these investigators was an amiable newsman named John Green. At first Green began to look into Sasquatch stories because he thought they might increase the circulation of the small newspaper he had just bought in Aggasiz, British Columbia. But he soon became the continent's most prodigious compiler of information on the subject, eventually turning the newspaper over to his wife so he could work full time on Sasquatch.

Retired logger Albert Ostman (at right in photo) claimed he had never heard of a Sasquatch until a 1924 camping trip in British Columbia— where, he says, he was held captive by a Sasquatch family for six days. Fearing ridicule, Ostman kept his experience secret until Bigfoot investigator René Dahinden (left) interviewed him in 1957.

Another enthusiast of the time was René Dahinden, a Swiss-born Canadian who pursued Sasquatch with such fervent single-minded purpose that it cost him his marriage. After more than thirty years of following the creature's tantalizing trails—sometimes in collaboration with Green—Dahinden would remain fiercely devoted to the search for Bigfoot. "Women?" he once scoffed to an interviewer, "I don't have time for them."

John Green's first Sasquatch story appeared on April 1, 1955. A fanciful account of a hairy giant carrying off a

young woman from a spa in nearby Harrison Hot Springs, it was in fact an April Fool's Day joke. But the Aggasiz town fathers were sufficiently amused that when they later had to come up with a local way to celebrate the British Columbia centennial, they decided to sponsor a mock Sasquatch hunt. This good-natured spoof drew light-hearted attention from the international press—and a serious visit from the earnest René Dahinden, who was embarrassed to learn that the hunt was all in fun.

But the fanfare also put Green in touch with a number of local people who did not think Sasquatch was a joke at all. He heard from people who seemed reliable and had seen huge, humanlike tracks, measuring as much as sixteen inches by eight inches, in the region. And he also obtained the sworn statement of a trapper named William Roe, who had been poking around a deserted gold mine near Jasper, Alberta, that year and had encountered what at first he took to be a grizzly bear.

"Then I saw it was not a bear," said Roe. "My first impression was of a huge man, about six feet tall, almost three feet wide and probably weighing somewhere near 300 pounds. It was covered from head to foot with dark brown, silver-tipped hair." Roe watched unseen as the creature ap-

proached him—he could see now that it was a female—and, squatting, began to strip leaves from branches with her teeth, much as an ape might do.

Then it spotted Roe in the bushes. "A look of amazement crossed its face. Still in a crouched position, it backed up three or four short steps, then straightened up to its full height." At that, it walked away. Roe considered shooting the creature, but

In 1967, at Blue Creek Mountain in northern California, hundreds of tracks said to be those of a Bigfoot were found in an area being cleared for a new road (left). The largest prints, reported by expert René Dahinden (above) to be fifteen inches long, showed a stride of fifty-two inches. Investigators did not rule out a hoax, but concluded the tracks were probably from the feet of a living creature.

it seemed so human that he could not bring himself even to raise his rifle, much less to fire. As it left, Roe said, the thing tipped its head back and emitted "a peculiar noise that seemed to be half laugh and half language."

Green was enthralled by such accounts and soon joined Dahinden in a concerted search for Sasquatch stories and evidence. One of their first team projects was a 1957 interview with a retired lumberman, Albert Ostman, who agreed to tell them a fantastic story that he claimed to have kept to himself for thirty-three years.

During a vacation in 1924, Ostman related, he had decided to do some gold prospecting near Toba Inlet, opposite Vancouver Island, and set up a campsite near a spring. On two successive mornings, he arose to find that his gear had been tampered with—most likely, he surmised, by a porcupine. He gave the matter little thought, although he decided to stow his cooking equipment and some other supplies in his sleeping bag for safekeeping. But on the third night, said Ostman, he awoke in panic as he was picked up bodily in his sleeping bag and carried away, extremely uncomfortable and nearly suffocated, for a distance that he guessed to be about twenty-five miles.

When he was set down, Ostman said, he struggled out of the sleeping bag only to find himself in a small, cliff-enclosed valley, being peered at by a family of enormous, hair-covered creatures, presumably Sasquatches. The family members—a huge, eight-foot-tall male, a seven-foot female, a young male of the same height, and a smaller female—chattered among themselves in a way that struck their uncomprehending captive as quite human. He was not harmed, the lumberman said, not even threatened, but neither was he allowed to leave.

"The hair on their heads was about six inches long," Ostman recalled. On the rest of their bodies it was "short, and thick in places." They had large feet with padded soles and wide hands with fingernails "like chisels." Ostman wrote that they were extremely agile, climbing rock faces with ease, except for the older female who had "very wide hips, and a gooselike walk." The young male of the family was fascinated by the pots and pans he had retrieved from the prospector's sleeping bag; he would also come close enough to take pinches of snuff from Ostman, which he would then hungrily eat. This "young fellow" had wide jaws and a narrow skull "that slanted upward round at the back about four or five inches higher than the forehead."

Ostman said that he remained in the valley with the supposed Sasquatches for six days before he managed to escape. His chance came when he enticed the old male into taking a can of snuff. The creature gulped down its entire contents and immediately became ill. In the confusion, Ostman fled, eventually reaching the coast and getting a boat back to civilization. He kept the incident a secret for so long, he said, because he feared being thought crazy or a liar. But by the late 1950s, Sasquatch accounts were becoming rather common—in no little part because a few people such as Green and Dahinden were taking them so seriously—and this encouraged Ostman to come forth and to tell his story at last.

In 1958, Green raced to the remote Bluff Creek area of northern California to check out a report from a bulldozer operator named Jerry Crew. Known to be a devout Baptist and teetotaler, Crew was working on a new road into a 17,000-square-mile wilderness area. One morning in August, Crew found his bulldozer surrounded by giant, humanlike tracks in the mud. Somewhat irritated by what he took to be a practical joke, he went about his road-building job. But when he found more tracks the next morning, and the morning after that, Crew asked his fellow workers to take a look. A few of the men had heard tales of giant, two-legged forest creatures. Some of his colleagues even claimed to have seen them in the area.

During the following two months, the road builders continued to find the tracks of creatures that had apparently circled the heavy equipment during the night, then stalked away into the surrounding ravines and gorges. With the as-sistance of a local hunter and taxidermist named Bob Titmus, who examined the tracks and declared that they were not made by any known animal, Crew made casts of one set of prints that were two inches deep and sixteen inches long. A newspaper in Eureka published the story on the front page, and Crew quickly became the subject of in-ternational attention.

Not long after John Green's arrival at Bluff Creek to investigate the story, he too found some tracks. And the stories coming in from the woods became more dramatic. One logger, Wilbur Wallace, reported following a trail of Sasquatch tracks down a steep hill from a work site and finding a fifty-five-gallon drum full of diesel oil 175 feet from the road. Judging from the tracks, the creature had picked up the barrel, carried it to the edge of the road, and hurled it over the side. Other equipment, such as a 250-pound truck tire, received the same treatment in ensuing days. Tracks were seen throughout the region, and a num-ber of people—including such presumably reliable witness-

In the most captivating frame of Roger Patterson's 1967 film, shot at a distance of about 130 feet, the purported Bigfoot briefly turns toward the camera. Researchers estimate the creature was just over six feet tall and weighed about 280 pounds.

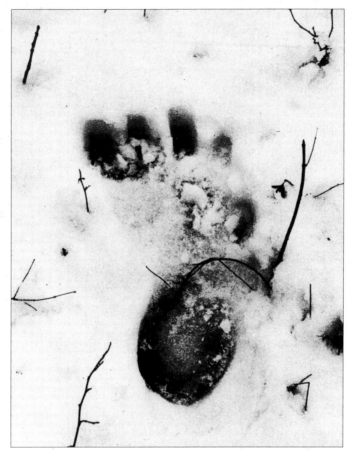

es as an expert hunter and two doctors—claimed to have caught glimpses of huge, hairy, bipedal creatures along back roads. When a reporter asked some Huppa Indians what the creatures might be, one old man said, "Good Lord, have the white men finally gotten around to that?"

It seemed clear that no ordinary man or known animal had made the tracks, with their walking stride of four feet and running stride of ten. Nor could any machine have negotiated the steep slopes they often ascended or descended. Perhaps the sightings, and the tracks as well, were hoaxes, yet there was no reason to suspect such a thing.

In the years that followed, the reports kept emanating from the Northwest. Like the Bluff Creek story, they remained inconclusive and unconfirmed by substantial evidence. Now and then, there would be an expedition; millionaire businessman Tom Slick, whose Yeti searches in the Himalayas had proved fruitless, organized one that was cut short by his death in a plane crash. For the most part, however, encounters with the Sasquatch continued to be fleeting and individual affairs.

Another one of them occurred at Bluff Creek, nine years after Crew made his plaster casts there. The result of the later incident was another set of casts—and Roger Patterson's famous twenty-four feet of film. Meanwhile, hairy giants were smelled, tracked, heard screaming, and even seen in many other parts of the United States—Ohio, Michigan, as far east as Maine. There were reports of a foul-smelling, humanlike monster called the Skunk Ape lurking in the swamplands of Florida, and similar stories from the remote, thicketed marshes along the Mississippi.

Then in the 1970s, a new—and, according to most cryptozoologists, utterly preposterous—explanation of the origins of such creatures began to emerge. In 1973, a sudden spate of Sasquatch sightings occurred in Westmoreland County, Pennsylvania, among other places in the East and Midwest. On September 27, for example, at about 9:30 p.m., two young girls awaiting a ride spotted a huge, hairy creature standing in the woods. The terrified girls ran home and described a white, eight-foot-tall monster with glowing red eyes that carried a luminous ball or sphere in one hand. Several people later reported that they had seen, that same night, what appeared to be a stationary aircraft hovering over the woods in the area, beaming a light down to the ground. The apparent connection between a rash of Sasquatch encounters and an outbreak of UFO sightings in the area led some to propose that Sasquatch was an extraterrestrial.

The idea seemed to gain support only a month later, near Greensburg, Pennsylvania, when a dozen people reported seeing a large, red UFO descending into a distant pasture. One young man (who used the pseudonym Stephen for his subsequent accounts of the episode) grabbed a rifle and drove off to investigate, along with two ten-year-old twin brothers. As they approached the pasture, the headlights of their car dimmed. They stopped and continued on foot until they crested a hill and saw a bright, dome-shaped craft about a hundred feet in diameter hovering just above the ground. They heard a low, humming noise and, from somewhere nearby, the sound of screaming.

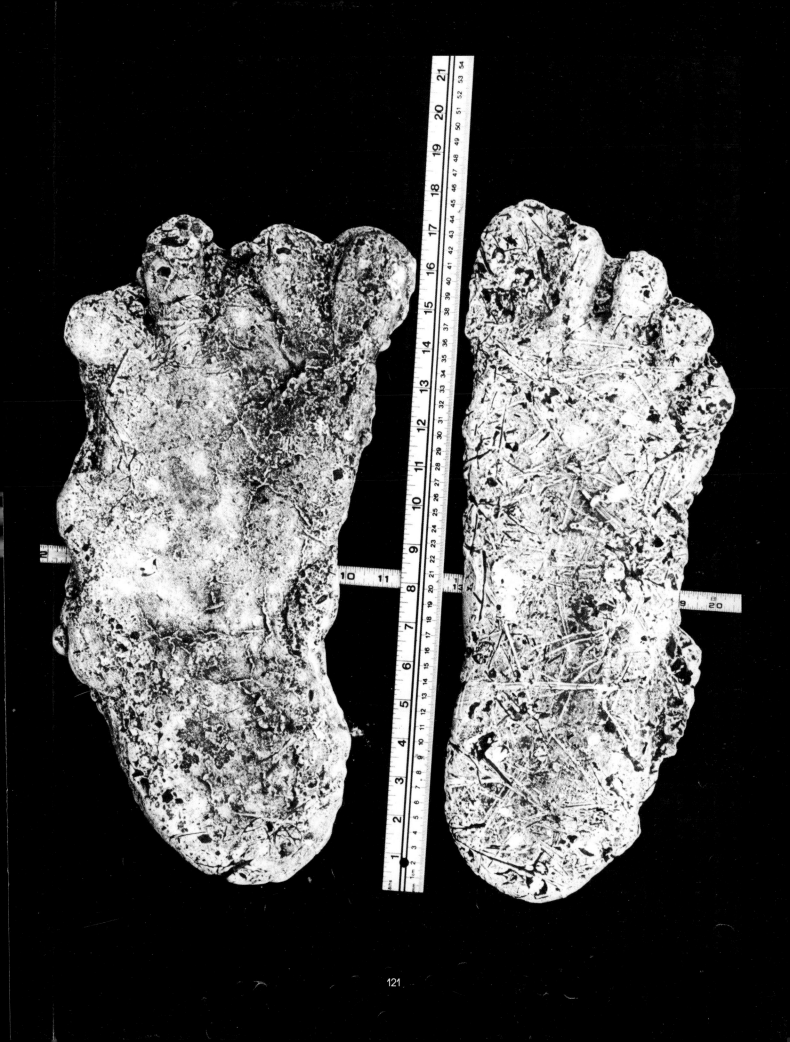

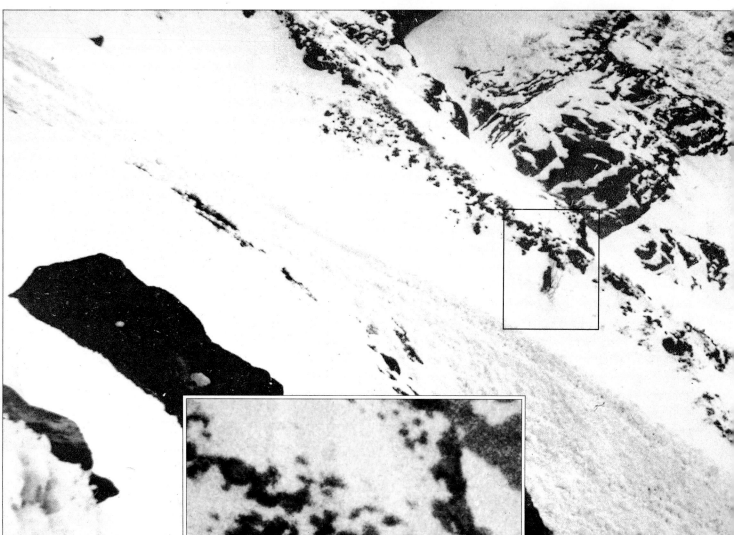

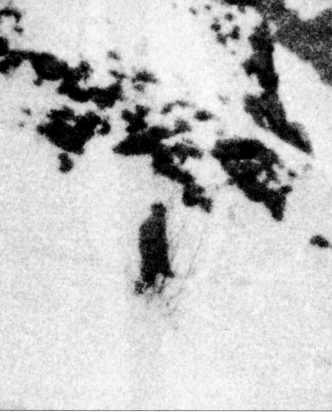

At that point, one of the twins called out in fear, having spotted something in the glow of the huge vehicle's light. Two apelike creatures, standing seven to eight feet tall, were lumbering toward them across the pasture. They had gray fur and glowing, green eyes. Twice Stephen fired over their heads, trying to scare them off, but they kept coming. One of the twins ran off in terror, while Stephen fired three rounds into the largest of the two creatures. It whined and raised its hands, and at that moment, the glowing bubblelike vehicle disappeared. The monsters walked away into the dark.

State police and UFO investigators who reached the scene later that night found no sign of monsters or a landing, but did encounter an unpleasant, sulfurous smell permeating the area. A number of investigators had difficulty breathing and became dizzy. Stephen's reaction was even more pronounced; he began to growl and flail his arms, shaking violently, at one point racing off around the field until he collapsed.

Such reported sightings of Sasquatch-like creatures and UFOs at the same time are relatively rare, though persistent, particularly in the Midwest. It is no surprise that they have led to the formulation of some bizarre theories. One of these is that UFOs are the products of electromagnetic energy released by geological

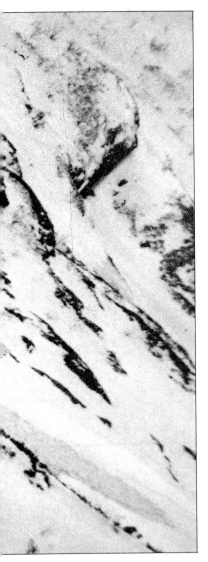

In March 1986, while peering across this barren landscape beyond an avalanche of snow that had swept over a Himalayan trail only moments before he arrived, Anthony Wooldridge spotted what he took to be the erect figure of a Yeti (inset). But Wooldridge later concluded that the supposed Yeti was probably a rock.

stress deep in the earth; this energy, playing on the brain, creates images of UFOs, and by the same process could produce Sasquatch hallucinations.

A less-benign variant of that scenario has been offered by a magician and UFO writer named John Keel. He has suggested that the creatures reported in the vicinity of landed UFOs materialize by drawing energy from the witness, in a kind of bloodless vampirism, emerging into our world fleetingly from some other dimension. According to Keel, this phenomenon could explain the continuing elusiveness of Sasquatch, the chief physical evidence of which consists of some 1,500 tracks leading nowhere.

Such theorizing may be dismissed easily enough, but the existence of so many tracks was evidence enough to lead at least one well-known member of the scientific establishment to proclaim the reality of Sasquatch. John Napier, a British anatomist and anthropologist who had served as the Smithsonian Institution's director of primate biology in the 1960s and was later a professor at the University of London, made a thorough study of the evidence for such creatures. In 1973 he published his findings in *Bigfoot: The Yeti and Sasquatch in Myth and Reality.*

To Napier, the evidence for Sasquatch was all but overwhelming. "No one doubts that some of the footprints are hoaxes and that some eyewitnesses are lying," he conceded, "but if *one* track and *one* report is true-bill, then myth must be chucked out the window and reality admitted through the front doors." The weight of the evidence convinced him, he declared, that "some of the tracks are real," and that "Sasquatch exists."

While Napier was sympathetic to the claims for the Yeti, his scientific caution barred him from taking them at face value. The effects of melting snow on footprints, the relative vagueness of sighting reports, and the Sherpa belief in the dual nature of reality led Napier, like Edmund Hillary, to dismiss the Yeti "as a red herring, or, at least as a red bear." A single piece of evidence—Shipton's clear if enigmatic footprint from the 1950s—continued to bother Napier, but he insisted nevertheless that the Yeti still remained to be shown as real.

Thirteen years after his book appeared, Napier saw what seemed to be convincing proof that the Yeti did indeed exist. The new and tantalizing evidence came from an Englishman named Anthony B. Wooldridge. Early one morning in March 1986, Wooldridge was in the Himalayas of northern India, close to the Nepalese border. At about 11,000 feet, he came across "strange tracks" in the snow, measuring some ten inches long. Wooldridge pressed on until, about 2,000 feet higher, he found that his progress up the incline was blocked by the remains of an avalanche of wet snow. Moving closer to the impassable snow pile, he discovered additional tracks on the other side, leading across a slope to a small bush. Behind the bush, steady and motionless, was what appeared to be an erect creature standing six or more feet tall.

"The head was large and squarish," Wooldridge reported later, "and the whole body seemed to be covered with dark hair." He was able to get to within about 500 feet of the presumed creature, which remained unmoving by the bush, and photographed it with his Nikon camera. Then, after observing the startlingly humanlike figure for some forty-five minutes, Wooldridge noted that the weather was closing in and descended from the mountainside.

In England, he showed his photographs to a number of scientists, among them zoologist Desmond Morris, a skeptic when it came to Yetis. Morris found the pictures "puzzling." Napier was less restrained. "In my view," he

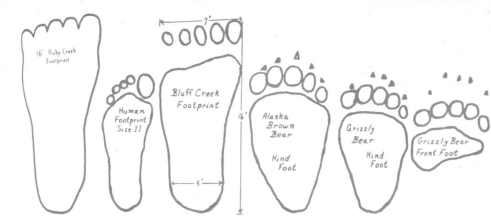

Supposed tracks of Bigfoot have often been dismissed as large human prints, bear tracks, or hoaxes. But a comparison of Bigfoot tracks with human and bear prints, shown above in comparative scale, suggests clear differences.

wrote, "the creature in the photograph is a hominid. . . . The creature cannot be anything but a Yeti."

The Wooldridge photographs are indeed convincing, appearing to show a humanlike figure standing at apparent ease beside a mountainside bush *(pages 122-123)*. But such pictures are not always what they seem. In late 1987, not long after John Napier died of a stroke, Wooldridge announced forthrightly that painstaking analysis of his Himalayan photographs, and comparisons with pictures taken later of the same scene, had shown that "the object photographed was almost certainly a rock."

Although Wooldridge's photographs yielded up their mystery relatively quickly, the same cannot be said of Roger Patterson's enigmatic 1967 movie film of the female Sasquatch he supposedly encountered in the Pacific Northwest. The Patterson film has remained a focal point of the Sasquatch debate. If the film was a hoax, some investigators think, then Sasquatch need not be taken seriously, but if it was legitimate, then Sasquatch exists.

Napier was suspicious of the Patterson footage, finding the alleged Sasquatch's gait and general appearance somewhat unnatural. Another analyst, a British expert in biomechanics named Donald W. Grieve, concluded that if the film had been shot at the standard speed of 24 frames per second (fps), the creature it showed might actually have been a human in disguise. However, continued Grieve, the "possibility of fakery is ruled out if the speed of the film was 16 or 18 fps. In these conditions a normal human being could not duplicate the observed pattern."

Patterson, as it turned out, was uncertain about the speed setting of his camera. Ordinarily, he kept it at 24 fps, since that was more acceptable for use on television. But he remembered after his encounter with Sasquatch that the setting had been at 18 fps. Perhaps the speed had been accidentally changed when the spooked horse reared back in fright or when the camera was yanked so hurriedly from the saddlebag. Patterson, however, could not say for sure.

Later, Russian analysts in Moscow found a novel method of estimating the film speed. As Patterson had dashed toward the creature with his camera whirring, the film recorded how he had bobbed up and down with each step, thus recording the rate of his stride. The Russians calculated that if the film had been shot at 24 fps, then Patterson had been taking six steps per second—a faster pace by far than that of a world-class sprinter. According to the Russians, the film had to have been shot at 16 fps; according to Grieve, that would rule out a hoax.

Patterson died in 1972, but others continued to wrangle over his film. René Dahinden took it to some of the leading practitioners of cinematic deception in the world—the technicians at the Walt Disney studios. If the Sasquatch film was a hoax, said the cinematographers, it was a better hoax then even they could have created. Neither the Disney people nor any other analyst of the film has been able to find conclusive evidence of fraud—what movie people would refer to as "the zipper in the suit."

Further perspective on the famous film footage has come from Grover Krantz, a physical anthropologist at Washington State University. Krantz calculated that a creature of the Sasquatch's size and weight would require a foot quite different from a human's. It would have to be more flexible, he said, and the heel would have to extend farther back from the ankle. The Patterson film clearly shows the creature's projecting heel—an esoteric biomechanical detail that no former rodeo rider bent on a hoax could have been expected to know.

Krantz, whose pursuit of the elusive Sasquatch began in 1969, has studied many of the more than a thousand reports of sightings and has interviewed dozens of eyewitnesses. About half of them, he thinks, were "lying, were fooled by something else, saw something out of a whiskey bottle or gave me information too poor to evaluate. With the other half, I couldn't find anything wrong." Krantz has

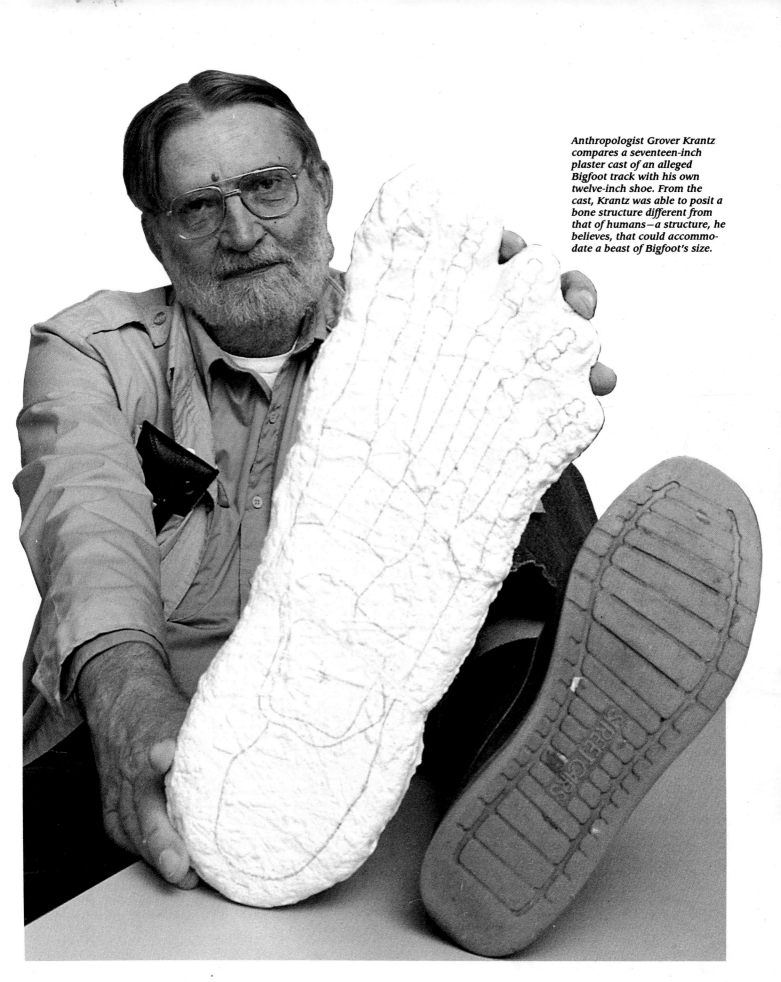

Anthropologist Grover Krantz compares a seventeen-inch plaster cast of an alleged Bigfoot track with his own twelve-inch shoe. From the cast, Krantz was able to posit a bone structure different from that of humans—a structure, he believes, that could accommodate a beast of Bigfoot's size.

125

also been impressed by more tangible evidence, such as that turned up in the spring of 1982 by Paul Freeman, a temporary employee of the U.S. National Forest Service.

On the morning of June 10, while tracking a small herd of elk along an old logging road near Walla Walla, Washington, Freeman spotted what he described as a Sasquatch-like figure descending an embankment about sixty yards ahead of him. The creature seemed to notice the human intruder and soon fled, but when Freeman and a party of fellow workers returned to investigate further, they discovered twenty-one well-defined footprints in the hard earth. The men made plaster casts of some of the tracks; six days later, while patrolling in the same general area, they found and made casts of another set of prints.

After examining the casts from both locations, Krantz determined that the tracks had been left by two individual creatures, each with feet about fifteen inches long. More intriguing, he found that the casts showed signs of dermal ridges—swirls of lines similar to fingerprints—and even sweat glands. According to Krantz, such minute detail could not be faked, a conclusion supported by several forensic and dermatological experts who studied the casts.

A number of other supposed Sasquatch tracks have been found in the Walla Walla area since 1982, leading Krantz to maintain that there are as many as six of the creatures ranging through the region. But if Krantz has no doubts about Sasquatch's reality, most scientists remain skeptical. Indeed, 88 percent of the North American university anthropology professors polled in a late-1970s survey would not even concede the possibility that such a creature might exist.

Photography is not conclusive, the scientists insist. There must be physical evidence—a carcass, a skull, or at least a handful of teeth. No one has suggested that Sasquatch is immortal, yet no bodies or even skeletons have ever been found. Hunters, though, respond that one rarely finds the remains of any large animal in the forest, because the bodies are disposed of and scattered very quickly by scavengers. The lack of fossil remains can also be ex-plained; there are few fossils of any kind to be found in the highly acidic soils of the Pacific Northwest.

For all that, there might have been a Sasquatch body to examine by now, were it not for the curious ethical problem the creature poses. Several people who have reported seeing a Sasquatch have said they were tempted to shoot it, but could not, because it seemed so human. In fact, Sasquatch is specifically protected by county ordinances in some jurisdictions.

Krantz, however, maintains that while the creature is surely a hominid, it is clearly not human—it lacks tools, clothes, fire, and language, as far as anyone can tell. For the sake of science, he argues, at least one of the beasts will have to be shot and brought in by the next searcher or hunter who happens to get the opportunity. However, despite the knowledge and understanding that would spring from such a find, the prospect raises daunting questions. Would the elusive Sasquatch be declared an endangered species? Would its forest habitat be protected? Would captured specimens be exhibited in zoos?

So far, such questions remain moot for all but a dedicated minority of travelers, adventurers, and scientists around the world. For them, the stories of what a privileged few have reportedly seen and heard and smelled, as well as the physical evidence recorded on scraps of film and in plaster casts, is enough. In all probability, they insist, those of us who venture into remote regions of the world are carefully observed and for the most part avoided by a large hominoid species—nocturnal, omnivorous, bipedal, and erect, rather like ourselves.

To these individuals, the planet earth remains a large place, retaining its mysteries and capable of surprises—in spite of all the efforts of civilized humans to put distance between themselves and their natural origins in the wild. There is room for giants, they say, not only in the universal myths of the monsters that came before us, but in the thickets of Oregon and the high forests of the Himalayas. If they have yet to prove their case, it is also true that they have yet to be proven wrong.

Monsters at the Matinee

"Hellllllllp meeeeeeeee!'' This plaintively futile cry, uttered as the spider bears down on the tiny man-bug at the climax of the movie *The Fly,* is just one in a gallery of terrifying moments that have thrilled generations of film audiences. From *Frankenstein* to *Alien,* movie monsters have clomped, slithered, and oozed across theater screens. These creatures, like the fanciful beasts of early myth, are often expressions of contemporary fears and uncertainties. Nuclear radiation, genetic engineering, and industrial pollution have all spawned their share of cinematic horrors, ranging from giant ants to humanoid plants and outsize bears *(pages 128-137).*

Although the monsters themselves come in all shapes and sizes, certain dramatic conventions seem to govern most movies in which their stories unfold. Often, for instance, misguided or deranged scientists are responsible for the monstrosity, and it is a safe bet that they will fall prey to the beast by the final reel. Benign scientists, on the other hand, sometimes have attractive and brainy daughters who are rescued by—and fall in love with—the handsome, square-jawed hero who contrives to triumph over the threatening creature.

But the audience can rarely assume that such couples will live happily ever after. Experience has shown that movie monsters are notoriously hard to kill. Usually, they are not dead at all; they are merely lurking at bay, healing their wounds, plotting their revenge, and waiting for a sequel.

Atomic Ants

In the pioneering film *Them!* radiation from an atomic bomb creates a swarming horde of gigantic killer ants in the New Mexico desert. The FBI teams up with two leading entomologists and manages to destroy the creatures before they can infest the storm drains of Los Angeles.

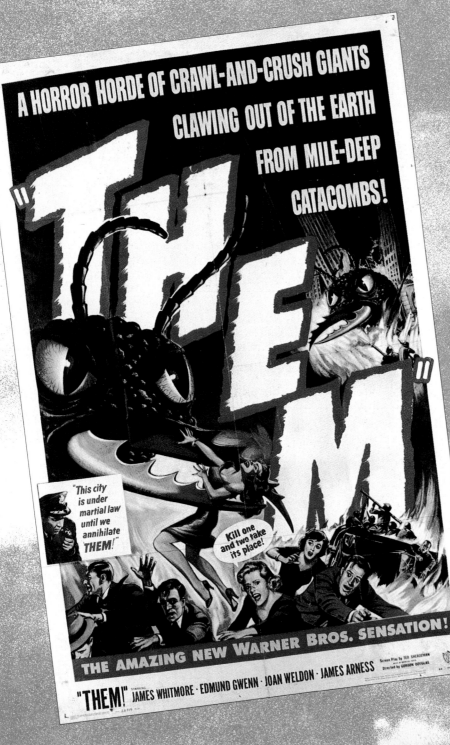

A Monster from the Past

Atomic weaponry wreaks unexpected havoc in *The Beast from 20,000 Fathoms* when a test explosion in the Arctic revives a slumbering prehistoric "rhedo-saurus." Devouring policeman and paleontologist alike, sowing panic in its path, the creature threatens to level New York City, where skyscrapers rise from the site of its ancient breeding ground.

A Human Fly

An experiment in matter trans-
ference goes dreadfully
wrong in *The Fly* as scientist
André Delambre suddenly finds
himself with the head and
forelimb of the title insect. As his
wife frantically searches for
a way to reverse the process, the
hapless André begins to realize
that his mind as well as his body
has been affected by the hideous "scrambling of atoms."

The Plant People

Believing that the survival of civilization depends on successfully crossbreeding human beings with plant life, a deranged scientist engineers a series of increasingly bizarre hybrid creatures in *The Mutations*. The scientist meets a gruesome end when his daughter's fiancé, furious at having been transformed into a human Venus's-flytrap, hungers for revenge.

Mutations in Maine

Reports of environmental hazards produced by a lumber mill bring investigator Robert Vern to the backwoods of Maine, where he encounters a number of fearsome mutations—including oversize fish and a rampaging bearlike beast. Vern manages to triumph over the killer animals—temporarily, at least—but *Prophecy*. leaves unresolved the nightmarish issues of industrial pollution.

ACKNOWLEDGMENTS

The index was prepared by Hazel Blumberg-McKee. The editors wish to thank these individuals and institutions for their valuable assistance in the preparation of this volume. René Dahinden, Richmond, British Columbia; Anthony G. Harmsworth, Loch Ness Centre, Drumnadrochit, Scotland; Bernard Heuvelmans, Centre de Cryptozoologie, Le Vésinet, France; Melissa Hough, CIGNA Museum and Art Collection, Philadelphia, Pennsylvania; Fridolf Johnson, Woodstock, New York; Dr. Roy P. Mackal, Chicago, Illinois; Dr. Clyde Roper, National Museum of Natural History, Smithsonian Institution, Washington, D.C.; Dottie Schneider, Philadelphia, Pennsylvania.

BIBLIOGRAPHY

Adamnan, Ninth Abbot of Hy, *Life of Saint Columba.* Ed. by William Reeves. Edinburgh: Edmonston and Douglas, 1874.

"Are There Sea Serpents, Really?" *New York Herald-Tribune,* August 14, 1955.

Aylesworth, Thomas G., *Science Looks at Mysterious Monsters.* New York: Julian Messner, 1982.

Bauer, Henry H., *The Enigma of Loch Ness.* Urbana, Ill.: University of Illinois Press, 1986.

Baumann, Elwood D., *The Loch Ness Monster.* New York: Franklin Watts, 1972.

Bayanov, Dmitri, "A Field Investigation into the Relict Hominoid Situation in Tajikistan, U.S.S.R." *Cryptozoology,* Vol. 3, 1984.

Bendick, Jeanne, *The Mystery of the Loch Ness Monster.* New York: McGraw-Hill, 1976.

Binns, Ronald, *The Loch Ness Mystery Solved.* Buffalo: Prometheus Books, 1984.

Bishop, Barry C., "Wintering in the High Himalayas." *National Geographic,* October 1962.

Boffey, Philip M., " 'Chessie' Back in the Swim Again." *New York Times,* September 4, 1984.

Bonington, Chris, *Annapurna South Face.* New York: McGraw-Hill, 1971.

Bord, Janet, and Colin Bord:
   The Bigfoot Casebook. Harrisburg, Pa.: Stackpole Books, 1982.
   The Evidence for Bigfoot and Other Man-Beasts. Ed. by Hilary Evans. Wellingborough, Northamptonshire, England: Aquarian Press, 1984.

Bright, Michael, "Meet Mokele-Mbembe." *BBC Wildlife,* December 1984.

Byrne, Peter, *The Search for Big Foot.* New York: Pocket Books, 1976.

Campbell, Elizabeth Montgomery, and David Solomon, *The Search for Morag.* New York: Walker and Company, 1973.

Campbell, Steuart, *The Loch Ness Monster: The Evidence.* Wellingborough, Northamptonshire, England: Aquarian Press, 1986.

Cohen, Daniel:
   The Encyclopedia of Monsters. New York: Dodd, Mead, 1982.
   A Modern Look at Monsters. New York: Dodd, Mead, 1970.

Cooke, David C., and Yvonne Cooke, *The Great Monster Hunt.* New York: W. W. Norton, 1969.

Costello, Peter, *In Search of Lake Monsters.* New York: Coward, McCann & Geoghegan, 1974.

"Coverage in Depth." *Time,* June 21, 1976.

DeYoung, Karen, "Sonar Search for 'Nessie' Reveals 3 Wobbly Scratches." *Washington Post,* October 11, 1987.

Dinsdale, Tim:
   Loch Ness Monster. London: Routledge & Kegan Paul, 1982.
   Monster Hunt. Washington, D.C.: Acropolis Books, 1972.
   Project Water Horse: The True Story of the Monster Quest at Loch Ness. London: Routledge & Kegan Paul, 1975.

Ellis, William S., "Loch Ness: The Lake and the Legend." *National Geographic,* June 1977.

Geist, William E., "Village on Lake Champlain Seeking Its Fortune in Tale of a Fabulous Sea Monster." *New York Times,* November 29, 1980.

Gould, R. T.:
   The Case for the Sea-Serpent. Detroit: Singing Tree Press, 1969 (reprint of 1930 edition).
   The Loch Ness Monster and Others. London: Geoffrey Bles, 1934.

Green, John:
   On the Track of the Sasquatch. Agassiz, B.C., Canada: Cheam Publishing, 1968.
   Sasquatch: The Apes among Us. Seattle: Hancock House, 1978.
   The Sasquatch File. Agassiz, B.C., Canada: Cheam Publishing, 1973.
   Year of the Sasquatch. Agassiz, B.C., Canada: Cheam Publishing, 1970.

Gregory, William K., "The Loch Ness 'Monster'." *Natural History,* April 1980.

Grumley, Michael, *There Are Giants in the Earth.* Garden City, N.Y.: Doubleday, 1974.

Haining, Peter, *Ancient Mysteries.* New York: Taplinger Publishing, 1977.

Halpin, Marjorie M., and Michael M. Ames, eds., *Manlike Monsters on Trial: Early Records and Modern Evidence.* Vancouver, B.C., Canada: University of British Columbia Press, 1980.

Harper, Jennifer, "Keeping the Monster Watch." *Washington Times Magazine,* July 17, 1986.

Heaney, Michael, "The Mongolian Almas: A Historical Reevaluation of the Sighting by Baradiin." *Cryptozoology,* Vol. 2, 1983.

Helm, Thomas, *Monsters of the Deep.* New York: Dodd, Mead, 1966.

Helton, David, "The Creature from the Avalanche." *BBC Wildlife,* September 1986.

Heuvelmans, Bernard:
   In the Wake of the Sea-Serpents. Transl. by Richard Garnett. New York: Hill and Wang, 1965.
   On the Track of Unknown Animals. Transl. by Richard Garnett. New York: Hill and Wang, 1958.

Hewkin, James A., "Investigating Sasquatch Evidence in the Pacific Northwest." *Cryptozoology,* Vol. 5, 1986.

Hillary, Sir Edmund, and Desmond Doig, *High in the Thin Cold Air.* Garden City, N.Y.: Doubleday, 1962.

Holiday, F. W., *The Great Orm of Loch Ness: A Practical Inquiry into the Nature and Habits of Water-Monsters.* New York: W. W. Norton, 1969.

Hunter, Don, with René Dahinden, *Sasquatch.* Toronto: McClelland and Stewart, 1973.

Huyghe, Patrick, "The Search for Bigfoot." *Science Digest,* September 1984.

International Society of Cryptozoology, *The ISC Newsletter.* Ed. by J. Richard Greenwell:
   "Champ Passes New York Assembly." Spring 1983.
   "Champ Photo Analysis Supports Animal Hypothesis." Autumn 1982.
   "Chesapeake Bay Monster Filmed on Videotape." Summer 1982.
   "Close Encounter in Lake Okanagan Revealed." Spring 1987.
   "Congo Expeditions Inconclusive." Spring 1982.
   "CSICOP Publishes Further Nessie Criticisms." Summer 1985.
   "Giant Octopus Blamed for Deep Sea Fishing Disruptions." Autumn 1985.
   "Interview with Paul H. LeBlond and Forrest G. Wood." Spring 1983.
   "Lake Champlain Monster Draws Worldwide Attention." Summer 1982.
   "Lake Champlain Update: 1983." Spring 1984.
   "Lloyds of London to Insure Ogopogo." Spring 1984.
   "Mokele-Mbembe: New Searches, New Claims." Autumn 1986.
   "Proposed Sasquatch Hunt Stirs New Controversies." Summer 1984.
   "Retouching of Nessie Flipper Photo Claimed—Denied." Winter 1984.
   " 'Sea Serpents' Seen off California Coast." Winter 1983.
   "Walla Walla Casts Show Dermal Ridges." Autumn 1982.

Izzard, Ralph, *The Abominable Snowman.* Garden City, N.Y.: Doubleday, 1955.

Joyner, Graham C., "The Orang-utan in England: An Explanation for the Use of Yahoo as a Name for the Australian Hairy Man." *Cryptozoology,* Vol. 3, 1984.

Krantz, Grover S., "Anatomy and Dermatoglyphics of Three Sasquatch Footprints." *Cryptozoology,* Vol. 2, 1983.

LeBlond, Paul H., and Michael J. Collins, "The Wilson Nessie Photo: A Size Determination Based on Physical Principles." *Cryptozoology,* Vol. 6, 1987.

LeBlond, Paul H., and John Sibert, "Observations of Large Unidentified Marine Animals in British Columbia and Adjacent Waters." Manuscript report no. 28 for the Institute of Oceanography, University of British Columbia, Vancouver, Canada.

Ley, Willy, *Exotic Zoology.* New York: Viking Press, 1959.

"Loch Ness: Something There?" *Science News,* April 17, 1976.

Lohr, Steve, "Myth or Fact, Nessie Is Still Luring Many." *New York Times,* October 11, 1988.

Lum, Peter, *Fabulous Beasts.* London: Thames and Hudson, 1952.

McCosker, John E., "Sandy, the Great White Shark." *Animal Kingdom,* December 1980/January 1981.

McEwan, Graham J.:
Mystery Animals of Britain and Ireland. London: Robert Hale, 1986.
Sea Serpents, Sailors and Sceptics. London: Routledge & Kegan Paul, 1978.

Mackal, Roy P.:
A Living Dinosaur? In Search of Mokele-Mbembe. Leiden, The Netherlands: E.J. Brill, 1987.
The Monsters of Loch Ness. Chicago: Swallow Press, 1980.
"Nessie's African Cousin." *Animal Kingdom,* December 1980/January 1981.
"The Search for Evidence of Mokele-Mbembe in the People's Republic of the Congo." *Cryptozoology,* Vol. 1, 1982.
Searching for Hidden Animals. Garden City, N.Y.: Doubleday, 1980.

Markotic, Vladimir, ed., *The Sasquatch and Other Unknown Hominoids.* Seattle: Hancock House, 1978.

Meredith, Dennis L., *Search at Loch Ness: The Expedition of the New York Times and the Academy of Applied Science.* New York: The New York Times Book Co., Quadrangle, 1977.

Moon, Mary, *Ogopogo: The Okanagan Mystery.* Vancouver, B.C., Canada: J. J. Douglas, 1977.

Napier, John, *Bigfoot: The Yeti and Sasquatch in Myth and Reality.* New York: E. P. Dutton, 1973.

Owen, Elizabeth, "In Search of a Monster." *Life,* August 1982.

Patterson, Roger, *Do Abominable Snowmen of America Really Exist?* Yakima, Wash.: Franklin Press, 1966.

Phillpotts, Beatrice, *Mermaids.* New York: Ballantine Books, 1980.

Poirier, Frank E., Hu Hongxing, and Chung-Min Chen, "The Evidence for Wildman in Hubei Province, People's Republic of China." *Cryptozoology,* Vol. 2, 1983.

Razdan, Rikki, and Alan Kielar, "Sonar and Photographic Searches for the Loch Ness Monster: A Reassessment." *The Skeptical Inquirer,* winter 1984-85.

"The (Retouched) Loch Ness Monster." *Discover,* September 1984.

Rines, Robert H., Harold E. Edgerton, and Robert Needleman, "Activities of the Academy of Applied Science Related to Investigations at Loch Ness, 1984." *Cryptozoology,* Vol. 3, 1984.

Roper, Clyde F. E., and Kenneth J. Boss, "The Giant Squid." *Scientific American,* April 1982.

Saar, John, "Salt-Water Nessie or Plesiosaurus, It's Back in the Briny." *Washington Post,* July 21, 1977.

Sanderson, Ivan T., *Abominable Snowmen: Legend Come to Life.* Philadelphia: Chilton, 1967.

"Search for Loch Ness Monster Comes Up Empty." Associated Press, October 12, 1987.

Searle, Frank, *Nessie: Seven Years in Search of the Monster.* London: Coronet Books, 1976.

Semple, Robert B., Jr., "Loch Ness Expedition, Switching Tactics, to Try Sonar Gear to Find Monster." *New York Times,* July 13, 1976.

Shackley, Myra, *Still Living?* New York: Thames and Hudson, 1983.

Shine, Adrian:
"Sounding Out the Sightings." *The Unexplained* (London), Vol. 1, Issue 12.
"To Catch a Monster." *The Unexplained* (London), Vol. 2, Issue 14.
"A Very Strange Fish?" *The Unexplained* (London), Vol. 2, Issue 13.

Sprague, Roderick, and Grover S. Krantz, eds., *The Scientist Looks at the Sasquatch II.* Vol. 4 of *Anthropological Monographs of the University of Idaho.* Moscow, Idaho: University Press of Idaho, 1979.

Sullivan, Walter, "Loch Ness Monster: A Serious View." *New York Times,* April 8, 1976.

Sweeney, James B.:
A Pictorial History of Sea Monsters and Other Dangerous Marine Life. New York: Crown Publishers, 1972.
Sea Monsters: A Collection of Eyewitness Accounts. New York: David McKay, 1977.

Tchernine, Odette, *In Pursuit of the Abominable Snowman.* New York: Taplinger Publishing, 1971.

Vachon, Brian, "Is There a Champlain Monster?" *Reader's Digest,* April 1978.

Waddell, L. A., *Among the Himalayas.* Ed. by H. K. Kuloy. Kathmandu, Nepal: Ratna Pustak Bhandar, 1978 (reprint of 1900 edition).

Wasson, Barbara, *Sasquatch Apparitions.* Bend, Oreg.: privately published, 1979.

Whyte, Constance, *More Than a Legend: The Story of the Loch Ness Monster.* London: Hamish Hamilton, 1957.

Wiley, John P., Jr., "Cameras, Sonar Close In on Denizen of Loch Ness." *Smithsonian,* June 1976.

Wilford, John Noble:
"Is It Lake Champlain's Monster?" *New York Times,* June 29, 1981.
"Scientists Plan All-Out Loch Ness Search." *New York Times,* May 28, 1976.
"Seekers of Loch Ness Monster Disappointed, Not Discouraged." *New York Times,* December 6, 1976.

Zarzynski, Joseph W., *Champ—Beyond the Legend.* Port Henry, N.Y.: Bannister Publications, 1984.

PICTURE CREDITS

Credits for the illustrations from left to right are separated by semicolons, from top to bottom by dashes.

Cover: Art by Alfred T. Kamajian. 7: Art by Bryan Leister, detail from page 15. 8-15: Art by Bryan Leister. 16, 17: Art by Wendy Popp. 18: Woodcut in *Mostri, Draghi e Serpenti: . . . di Ulisse Aldrovandi,* edited by Erminio Caprotti, published by Nuove Edizioni Gabriele Mazzotta, Milan—Mary Evans Picture Library, London—woodcut in *Mostri, Draghi e Serpenti: . . . di Ulisse Aldrovandi,* edited by Erminio Caprotti, published by Nuove Edizioni Gabriele Mazzotta, Milan—Mary Evans Picture Library, London. 19: Woodcuts in *Mostri, Draghi e Serpenti: . . . di Ulisse Aldrovandi,* edited by Erminio Caprotti, published by Nuove Edizioni Gabriele Mazzotta, Milan, except bottom right, Mary Evans Picture Library, London. 20, 21: David Doubilet; Wu Zuzheng/Photo Researchers, Inc.; © George Holton/Photo Researchers, Inc., 1971; Peter Davey/Bruce Coleman Inc.—© George Holton/Photo Researchers, Inc., 1978—© Tom McHugh/Photo Researchers, Inc., 1979. 23: Kohei Shinonoi/Uniphoto Press International Inc. 24: Fortean Picture Library, Wales. 25: Courtesy Dr. Clyde Roper. 26: Forbes Collection, Hart Nautical Collections, MIT Museum. 27: Boston Athenaeum. 29: Fortean Picture Library, Wales. 30: The Kendall Whaling Museum, Sharon, Massachusetts. 31: Culver Pictures. 32: Mary Evans Picture Library, London. 33: Illustrated London News Picture Library, London. 35, 36: Fortean Picture Library, Wales. 38: Courtesy International Society of Cryptozoology, Tucson, Arizona. 39: Art by Fred Holz. 40, 41: Fortean Picture Library, Wales—AP/Wide World Photos. 42: Fortean Picture Library, Wales. 43: AP/Wide World Photos. 45: Art by Lloyd K. Townsend, detail from page 50. 46-51: Art by Lloyd K. Townsend. 52, 53: Anadolu Medeniyetleri Müzesi, Ankara. 54: Lee Boltin, courtesy Fridolf Johnson, Woodstock, New York—woodcuts in *Mostri, Draghi e Serpenti: . . . di Ulisse Aldrovandi,* edited by Erminio Caprotti, published by Nuove Edizioni Gabriele Mazzotta, Milan (3). 55: Painting by John Archibald Woodside, Sr., courtesy CIGNA Museum and Art Collection, Philadelphia. 56: Michael Holford, Loughton/courtesy the Trustees of the British Museum, London; courtesy the Trustees of the British Museum, London. 57: From *Great Mysteries: Mysterious Monsters,* by Daniel Farson and Angus Hall, © Aldus Books, London, 1975; woodcut in *Mostri, Draghi e Serpenti: . . . di Ulisse Aldrovandi,* edited by Erminio Caprotti, published by Nuove Edizioni Gabriele Mazzotta, Milan; Bibliothèque Nationale, Paris—The Bodleian Library, Oxford. 58, 59: Mary Evans Picture Library, London; Nikos Kontos, Athens, courtesy Delphi Museum; Lee Boltin—Eckhard Ritter from Akademische Druck und Verlagsanstalt, Graz; Giraudon, Paris, courtesy Musée de Louvre, Paris. 61: Art by Wendy Popp. 62: Courtesy International Society of Cryptozoology, Tucson, Arizona. 63: Sandra Mansi/Gamma-Liaison. 64, 65: David Doubilet. 67: Map by Fred Holz based on map supplied by John Bartholemew and Son Ltd., Edinburgh. 68, 69: Popperfoto, London; Hugh Gray/Fortean Picture Library, Wales—Fortean Picture Library, Wales. 70: Ralph Izzard, Tunbridge Wells, Kent, from *The Hunt for the Buru,* Hodder and Stoughton, London, 1951. 72, 73: Terry Fincher/Photographers International, Guildford, Surrey. 74, 75: H. L. Cockrell/Camera Press, London; ITN; London/Tim Dinsdale; photograph by F. C. Adams, *Daily Mail,* London/Solo Syndication—R. K. Wilson/Fortean Picture Library, Wales—Lachlan Stewart/London Express News and Feature Service, from *More Than a Legend: The Story of the Loch Ness Monster,* by Constance Whyte, Hamish Hamilton, London, 1957; P. A. MacNab, courtesy Time Inc. Picture Collection. 76: Ivor Newby/National Archive, Loch Ness Centre, Drumnadrochit. 77: Courtesy Time Inc. Picture Collection. 78: © Academy of Applied Science, 1972, courtesy R. H. Rines. 79: © Academy of Applied Science, 1972. 80: Nicholas Witchell/Fortean Picture Library, Wales—© Academy of Applied Science, 1975. 81: © Academy of Applied Science, 1975/Syndication International, London. 82, 83: *Courtship in Loch Ness,* painting by Peter Scott, C.H., C.B.E., D.S.C., F.R.S., courtesy Christopher James, Isle of Mull, Scotland. 86, 87: David Doubilet. 88: Nicholas Witchell/Fortean Picture Library, Wales—Today/RDR Productions. 89: Today/RDR Productions. 91: Drawing by David Miller from *A Living Dinosaur? In Search of Mokele-Mbembe,* by Dr. Roy P. Mackal, © by E.J. Brill, Leiden, The Netherlands, 1987, detail from page 97. 92, 93: Marie T. Womack from *A Living Dinosaur? In Search of Mokele-Mbembe,* by Dr. Roy P. Mackal, © by E.J. Brill, Leiden, The Netherlands, 1987; map by William L. Hezlep. 94, 95: Background photograph by Dr. Roy P. Mackal, from *A Living Dinosaur? In Search of Mokele-Mbembe,* by Dr. Roy P. Mackal, © by E.J. Brill, Leiden, The Netherlands, 1987. Inset photographs by Justin Wilkinson from *A Living Dinosaur? In Search of Mokele-Mbembe,* by Dr. Roy P. Mackal, © by E.J. Brill, Leiden, The Netherlands, 1987; Dr. Roy P. Mackal from *A Living Dinosaur? In Search of Mokele-Mbembe,* by Dr. Roy P. Mackal, © by E.J. Brill, Leiden, The Netherlands, 1987—Marie T. Womack from *A Living Dinosaur? In Search of Mokele-Mbembe,* by Dr. Roy P. Mackal, © by E.J. Brill, Leiden, The Netherlands, 1987. 96, 97: Background photograph by Richard Greenwell, from *A Living Dinosaur? In Search of Mokele-Mbembe,* by Dr. Roy P. Mackal, © by E.J. Brill, Leiden, The Netherlands, 1987. Inset photograph courtesy International Society of Cryptozoology, Tucson, Arizona; drawing by David Miller from *A Living Dinosaur? In Search of Mokele-Mbembe,* by Dr. Roy P. Mackal, © by E.J. Brill, Leiden, The Netherlands, 1987. 99: Art by Wendy Popp. 101: Photothèque Musée de l'Homme, Paris. 102, 103: John Cleare/Mountain Camera, inset by Eric Shipton, courtesy the Royal Geographical Society Picture Collection, London. 104: *Daily Mail,* London/Solo Syndication. 105: UPI/Bettmann Newsphotos. 106: Myra Shackley, Bradford. 108, 109: Drawing by Lt. Col. V. S. Karapetian/Fortean Picture Library, Wales; from *Year of the Sasquatch,* by John Green, © Cheam Publishing Ltd., Saanichton, British Columbia, Canada, 1970. 111: Dr. Bernard Heuvelmans; courtesy International Society of Cryptozoology, Tucson, Arizona. 112: Courtesy International Society of Cryptozoology, Tucson, Arizona. 113: Dr. Zhou Guoxing/Fortean Picture Library, Wales. 114: From *Sasquatch: The Apes among Us,* by John Green, © Cheam Publishing Ltd., Saanichton, British Columbia, Canada, 1978; drawing by Robert Lea/Fortean Picture Library, Wales—Fortean Picture Library, Wales; drawing by Jack Cochran/Fortean Picture Library, Wales. 115: © James A. Sugar/Black Star, 1981. 116: © René Dahinden, Richmond, British Columbia, Canada, 1957. 117: René Dahinden/Fortean Picture Library, Wales. 118, 119: Patterson/Gimlin © René Dahinden, 1967. 120, 121: René Dahinden/Fortean Picture Library, Wales. 122, 123: A. B. Wooldridge, Altrincham. 124: From *Sasquatch: The Apes among Us,* by John Green, © Cheam Publishing Ltd., Saanichton, British Columbia, Canada, 1978. 125: Douglas Kirkland/Sygma. 127: © Warner Bros. Inc., 1953, 1981, all rights reserved, photograph courtesy Movie Star News, New York, detail from page 131. 128, 129 photomontage: Background, USAF Photographic Collection, National Air & Space Museum, Smithsonian Institution. Poster © Warner Bros. Inc., 1954, 1982, all rights reserved, photograph courtesy Crowell Beech; movie still © Warner Bros. Inc., 1954, 1982, all rights reserved. 130, 131 photomontage: Background, USAF Photographic Collection, National Air & Space Museum, Smithsonian Institution. Poster © Warner Bros. Inc., 1953, 1981, all rights reserved, photograph courtesy Kobal Collection, New York; movie still © Warner Bros. Inc., 1953, 1981, all rights reserved, photograph courtesy Movie Star News, New York. 132, 133 photomontage: Background, Fritz Goro for LIFE. Movie still from the Twentieth Century Fox Release THE FLY © 1958 Twentieth Century-Fox Film Corporation, all rights reserved, photograph courtesy Springer/Bettmann Film Archives, New York; poster from the Twentieth Century Fox Release THE FLY © 1958 Twentieth Century-Fox Film Corporation, all rights reserved. 134, 135 photomontage: Background, Fritz Goro. Poster and movie still © 1974 Getty Pictures Ltd., all rights reserved. 136, 137 photomontage: Background, John Zimmerman © 1967 Time-Life Books Inc. from *The Heartland* (Time-Life Library of America series). Movie still from PROPHECY © 1979 by Paramount Pictures Corporation, all rights reserved, photograph courtesy Movie Star News, New York; poster from PROPHECY © 1979 by Paramount Pictures Corporation, all rights reserved.

INDEX

Numerals in italics indicate an illustration of the subject mentioned.

Time-Life Books Inc.
is a wholly owned subsidiary of
TIME INCORPORATED

FOUNDER: Henry R. Luce 1898-1967

Editor-in-Chief: Jason McManus
Chairman and Chief Executive Officer: J. Richard Munro
President and Chief Operating Officer: N. J. Nicholas, Jr.
Editorial Director: Ray Cave
Executive Vice President, Books: Kelso F. Sutton
Vice President, Books: George Artandi

TIME-LIFE BOOKS INC.

EDITOR: George Constable
Executive Editor: Ellen Phillips
Director of Design: Louis Klein
Director of Editorial Resources: Phyllis K. Wise
Editorial Board: Russell B. Adams, Jr., Dale M. Brown,
Roberta Conlan, Thomas H. Flaherty, Lee Hassig, Donia
Ann Steele, Rosalind Stubenberg, Henry Woodhead
Director of Photography and Research:
John Conrad Weiser
Assistant Director of Editorial Resources: Elise Ritter Gibson

PRESIDENT: Christopher T. Linen
Chief Operating Officer: John M. Fahey, Jr.
Senior Vice Presidents: Robert M. DeSena, James L. Mercer,
Paul R. Stewart
Vice Presidents: Stephen L. Bair, Ralph J. Cuomo, Neal
Goff, Stephen L. Goldstein, Juanita T. James, Hallett
Johnson III, Carol Kaplan, Susan J. Maruyama, Robert H.
Smith, Joseph J. Ward
Director of Production Services: Robert J. Passantino

Editorial Operations
Copy Chief: Diane Ullius
Production: Celia Beattie
Library: Louise D. Forstall

17.45

Library of Congress Cataloging in Publication Data
Mysterious creatures.
  (Mysteries of the unknown).
  Bibliography: p.
  Includes index.
  1. Monsters. I. Time-Life Books.
QL89.M97 1988   001.9'44   88-2124
ISBN 0-8094-6332-6
ISBN 0-8094-6333-4 (lib. bdg.)

90B1266

MYSTERIES OF THE UNKNOWN

SERIES DIRECTOR: Russell B. Adams, Jr.
Series Administrator: Myrna Traylor-Herndon
Designer: Herbert H. Quarmby

Editorial Staff for *Mysterious Creatures*
Associate Editors: Jane N. Coughran (pictures);
Janet Cave (text)
Assistant Designer: Lorraine D. Rivard
Copy Coordinator: Mary Beth Oelkers-Keegan
Picture Coordinator: Betty H. Weatherley
Researchers: Scarlet Cheng, Christian D. Kinney,
Constance Strawbridge Contreras
Editorial Assistant: Donna Fountain

Special Contributors: Christine Hinze (London, picture
research); Laura Akgulian, Sarah Brash, George Daniels,
Martha Leff, Thomas A. Lewis, Jake Page, Marilynne R.
Rudick, Sandra Salmans, Daniel Stashower (text);
John Drummond (design); Vilasini Balakrishnan, Denise
Dersin, Anne Munoz-Furlong, Melva Holloman, Sharon
Obermiller, Patricia A. Paterno, Rhoda Christine Russell
(research)

Correspondents: Elisabeth Kraemer-Singh (Bonn), Vanessa
Kramer (London), Maria Vincenza Aloisi (Paris), Ann
Natanson (Rome).
Valuable assistance was also provided by Judy Aspinall
(London); Elizabeth Brown, Christina Lieberman (New
York).

The Consultants:
Marcello Truzzi, professor of sociology at Eastern
Michigan University, is also director of the Center for
Scientific Anomalies Research (CSAR) and editor of its
journal, the *Zetetic Scholar.* Dr. Truzzi, who considers
himself a "constructive skeptic" with regard to claims of
the paranormal, works through the CSAR to produce
dialogues between critics and proponents of unusual
scientific claims.

J. Richard Greenwell has served as secretary and editor of
publications for the International Society of Cryptozoology
since its founding in 1982 and is the author of *Animals
without Heritage,* a definitive work on obscure animals. In
his search for such creatures, he has done fieldwork in
two dozen countries, among them New Guinea and the
Congo.

Other Publications:

AMERICAN COUNTRY
VOYAGE THROUGH THE UNIVERSE
THE THIRD REICH
THE TIME-LIFE GARDENER'S GUIDE
TIME FRAME
FIX IT YOURSELF
FITNESS, HEALTH & NUTRITION
SUCCESSFUL PARENTING
HEALTHY HOME COOKING
UNDERSTANDING COMPUTERS
LIBRARY OF NATIONS
THE ENCHANTED WORLD
THE KODAK LIBRARY OF CREATIVE PHOTOGRAPHY
GREAT MEALS IN MINUTES
THE CIVIL WAR
PLANET EARTH
COLLECTOR'S LIBRARY OF THE CIVIL WAR
THE EPIC OF FLIGHT
THE GOOD COOK
WORLD WAR II
HOME REPAIR AND IMPROVEMENT
THE OLD WEST

*For information on and a full description of any of the
Time-Life Books series listed above, please call 1-800-
621-7026 or write:*
  Reader Information
  Time-Life Customer Service
  P.O. Box C-32068
  Richmond, Virginia 23261-2068

This volume is one of a series that examines the history
and nature of seemingly paranormal phenomena. Other
books in the series include:
Mystic Places
Psychic Powers
The UFO Phenomenon
Psychic Voyages
Phantom Encounters
Visions and Prophecies

Time-Life Books Inc. offers a wide range of fine record-
ings, including a *Rock 'n' Roll Era* series. For subscription
information, call 1-800-621-7026 or write Time-Life
Music, P.O. Box C-32068, Richmond, Virginia 23261-2068.